MANDALA

COLORING BOOK FOR ADULT
RELAXATION

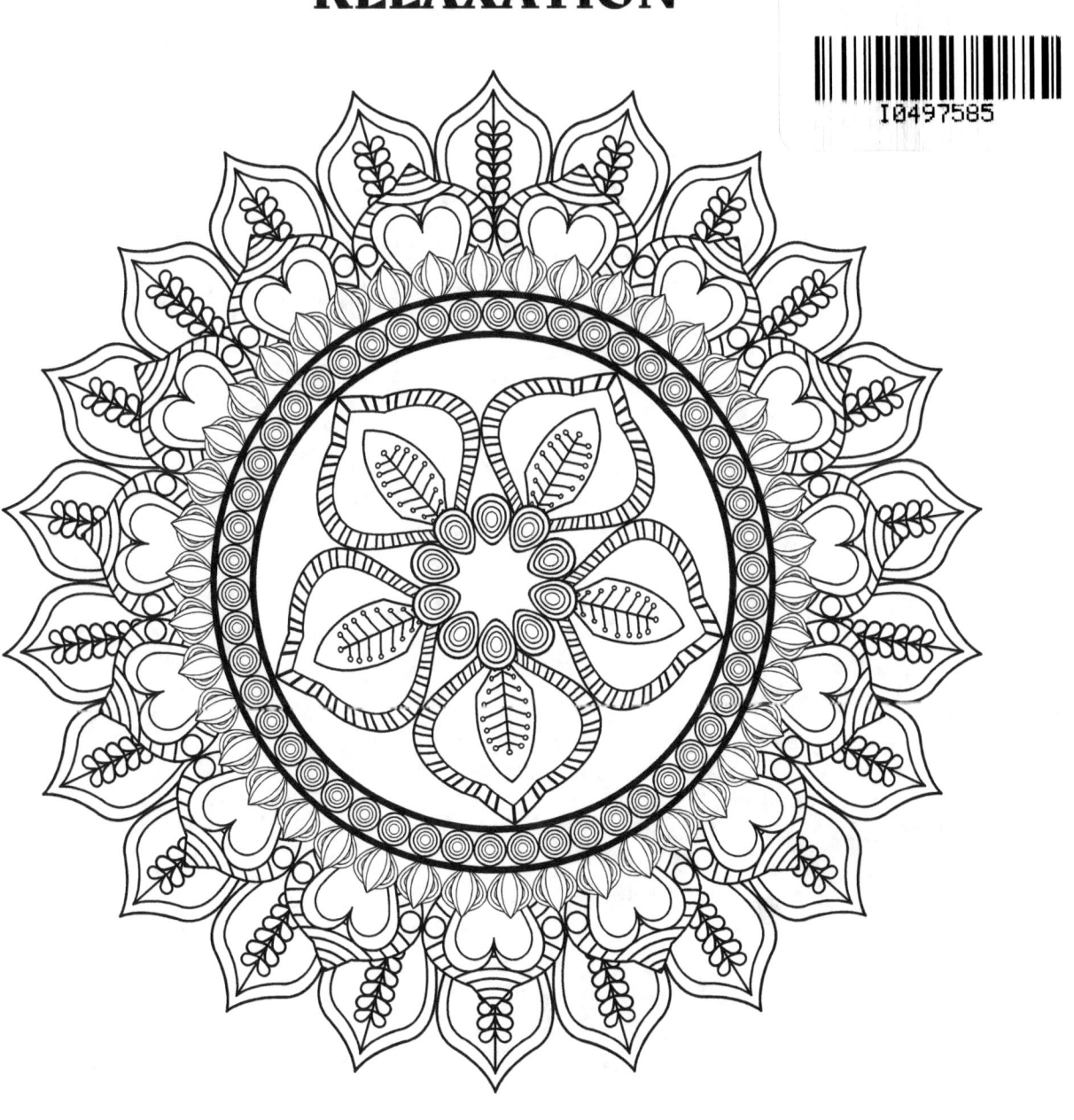

**Copyright © 2020 by
Royal Coloring Book**

All rights reserved. No portion of this book may be reproduced in any form or any means including photocopy. Recording or electronic mechanical methods without permission from the publisher. Except as permitted by copyright law.

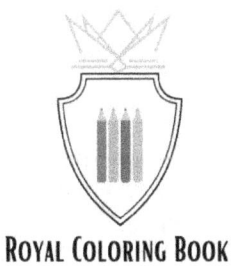

ROYAL COLORING BOOK

COLOR TEST PAGE

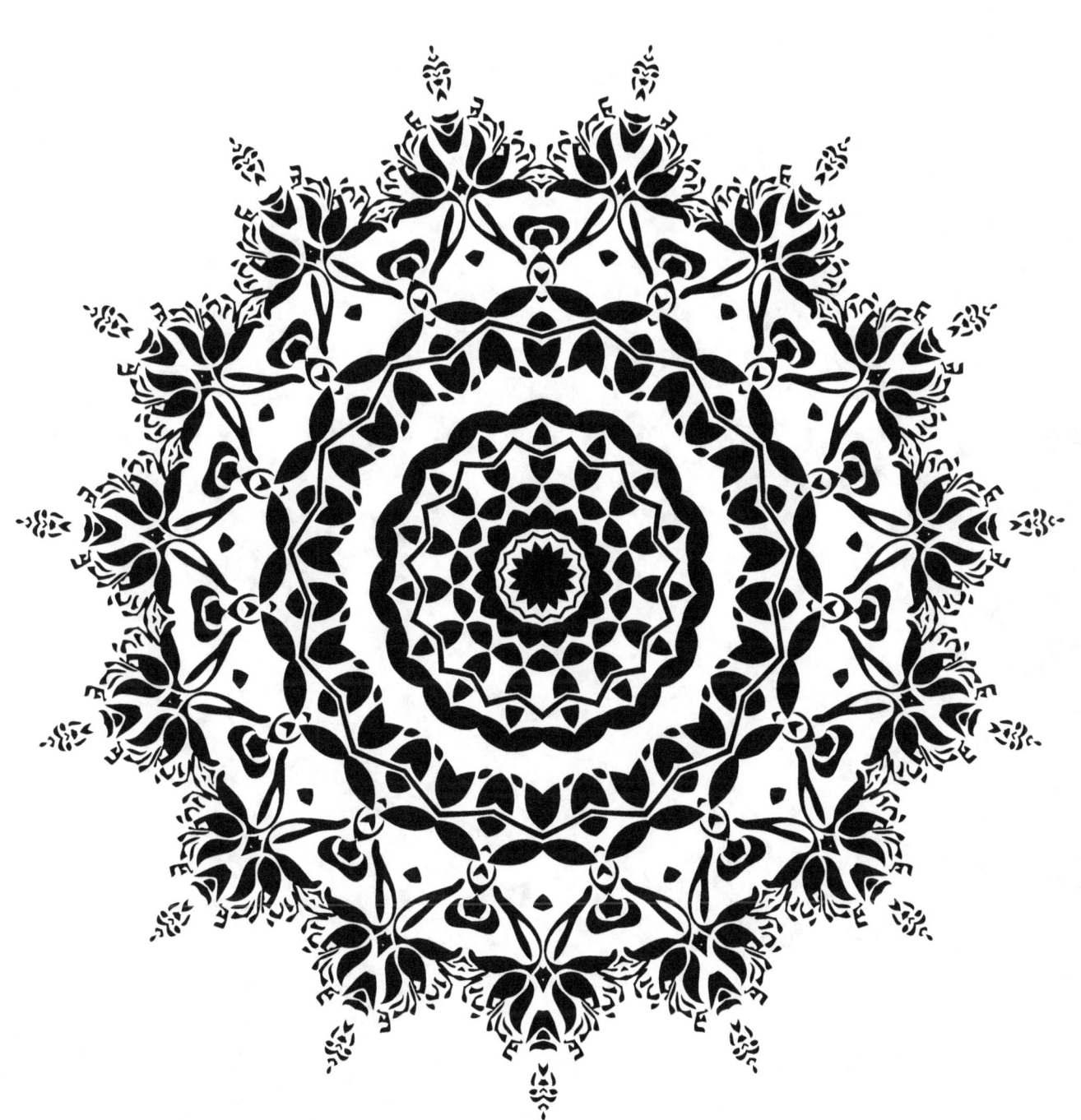

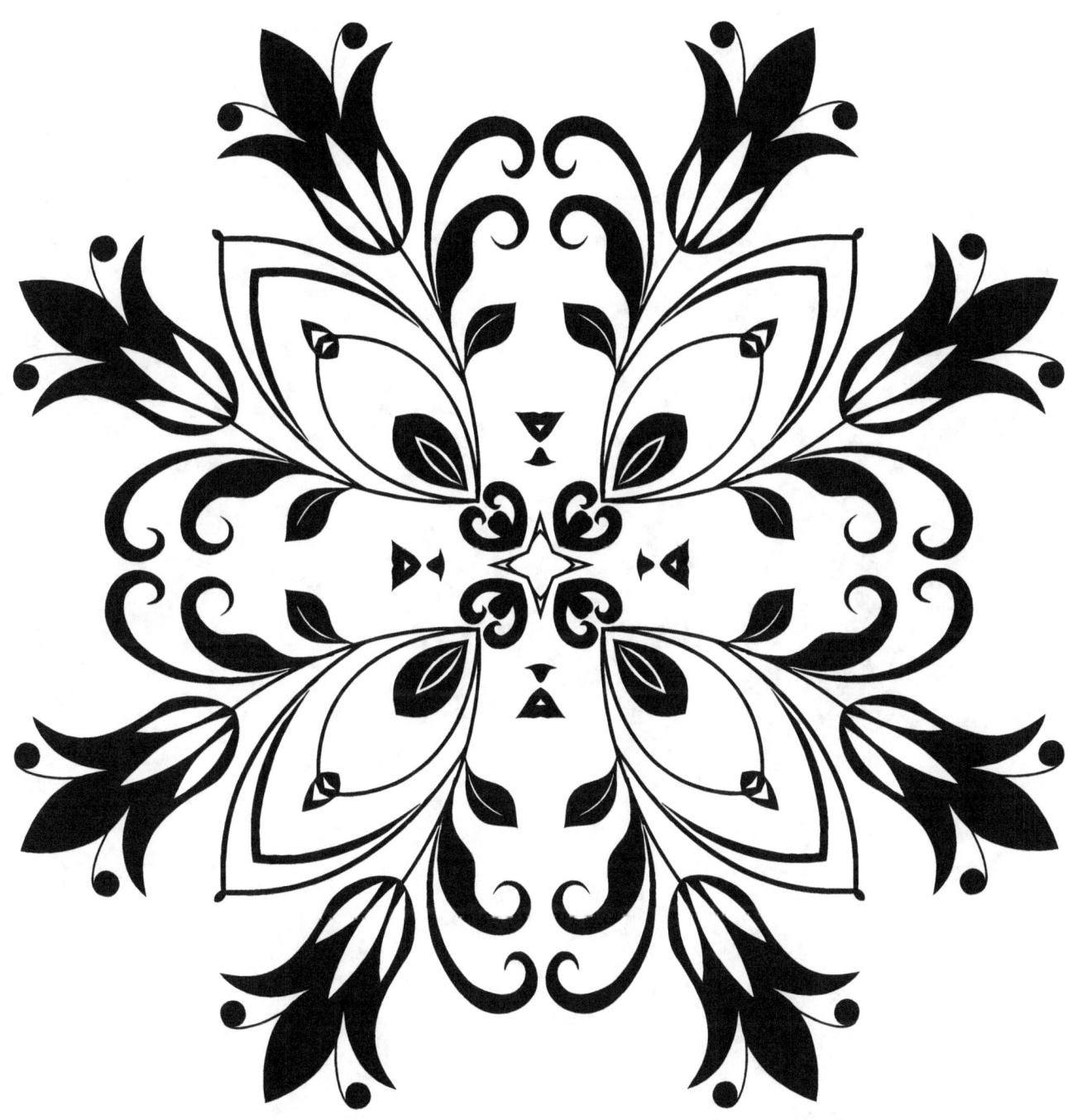

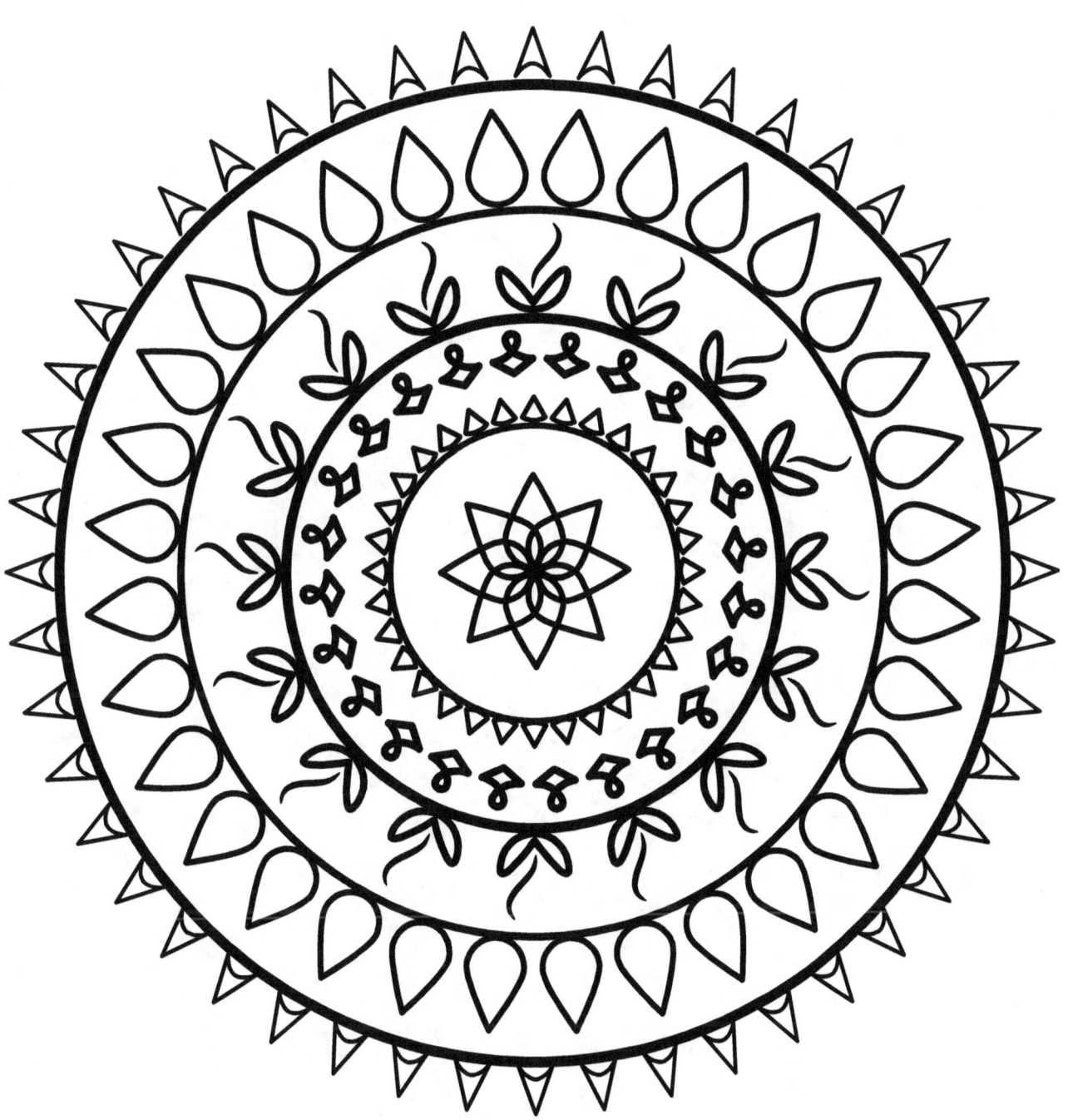

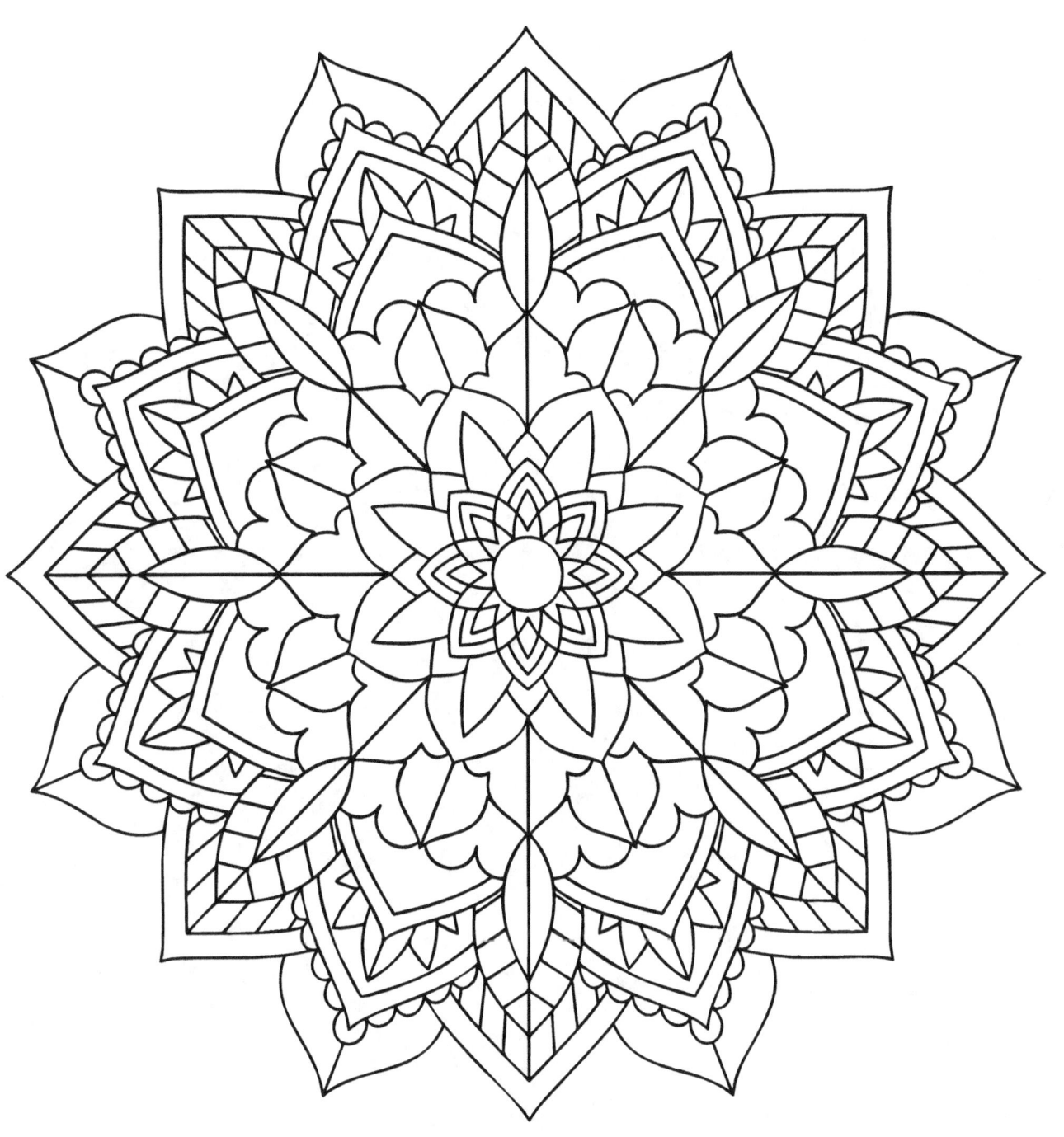

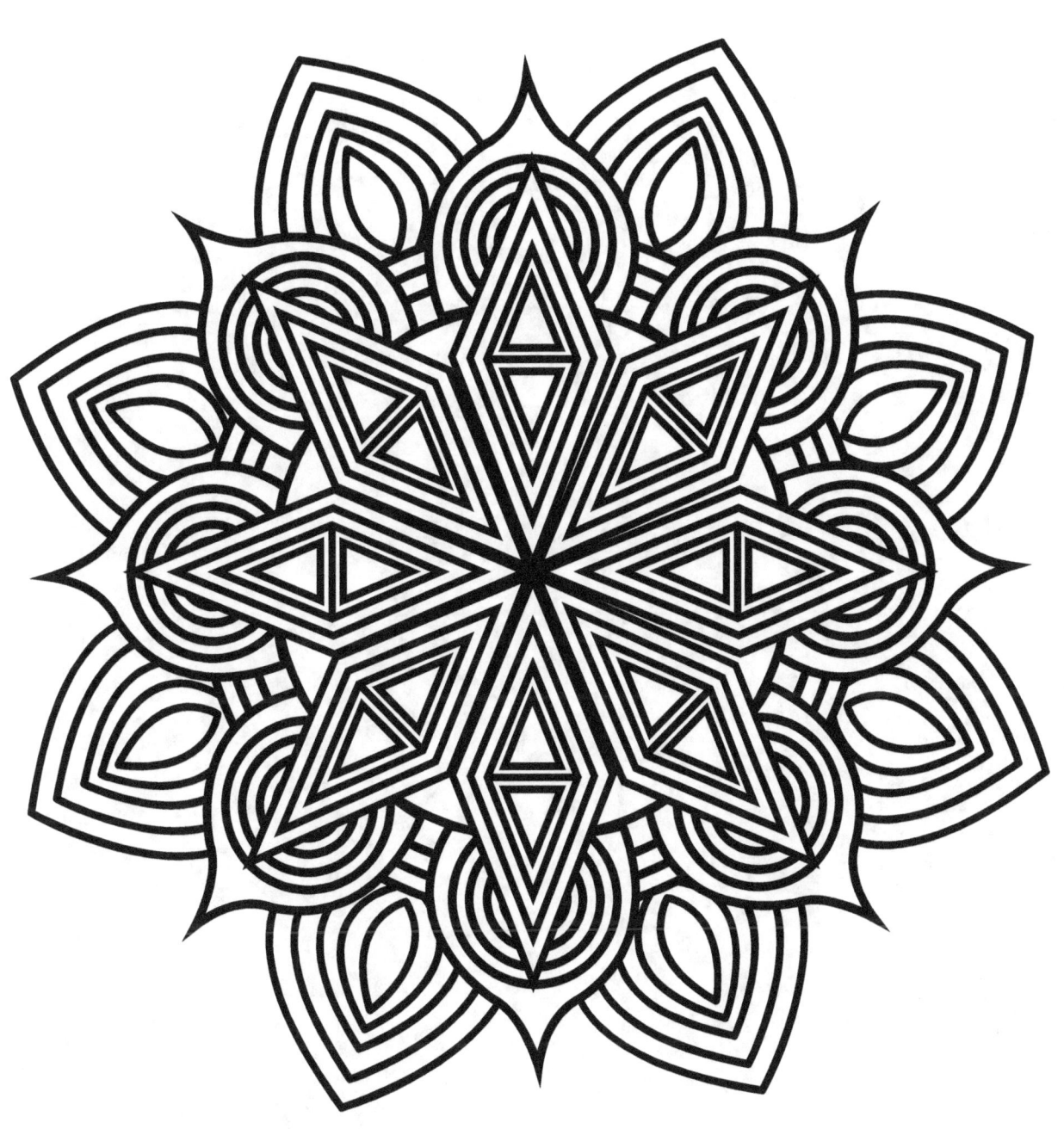

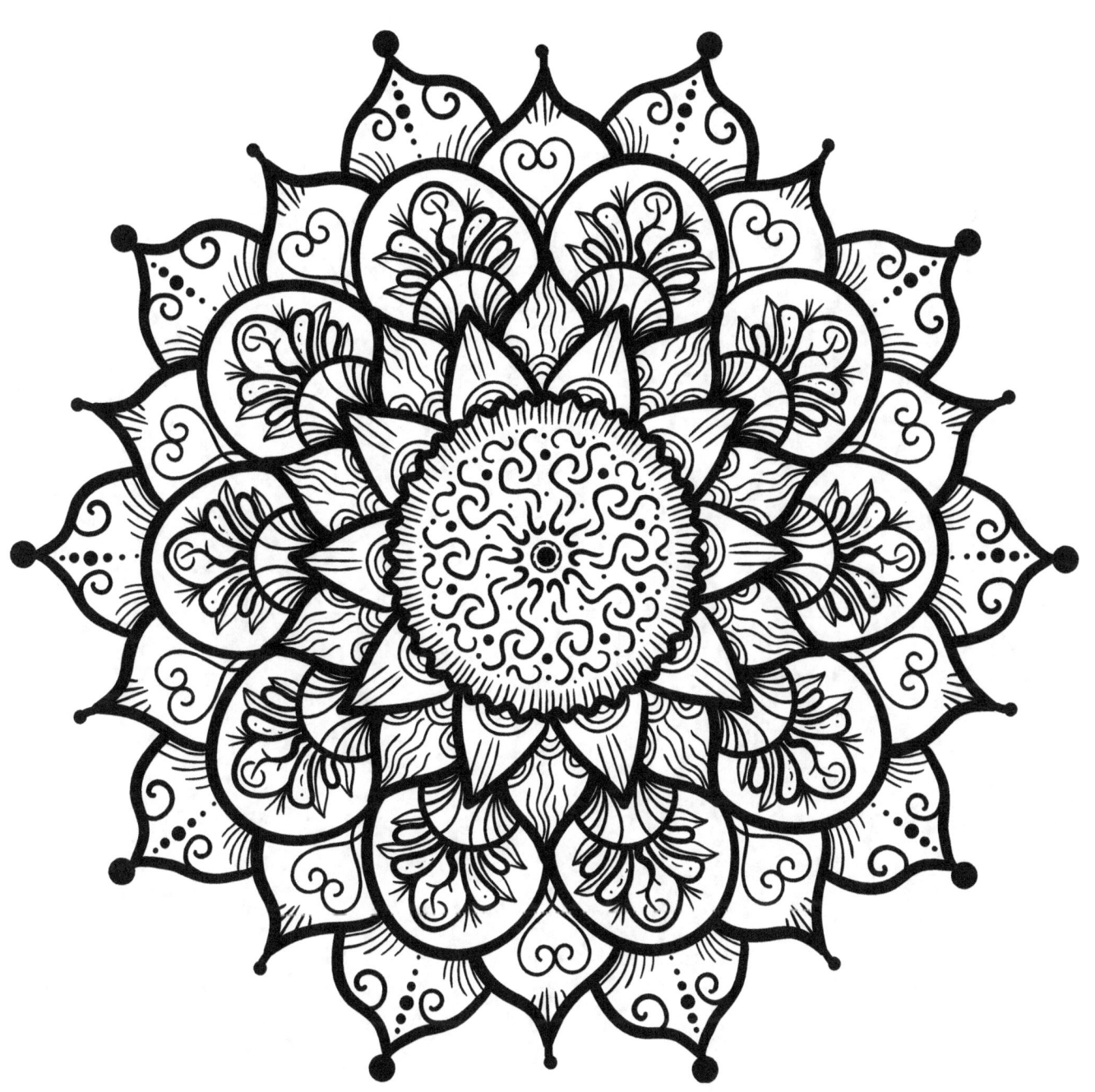

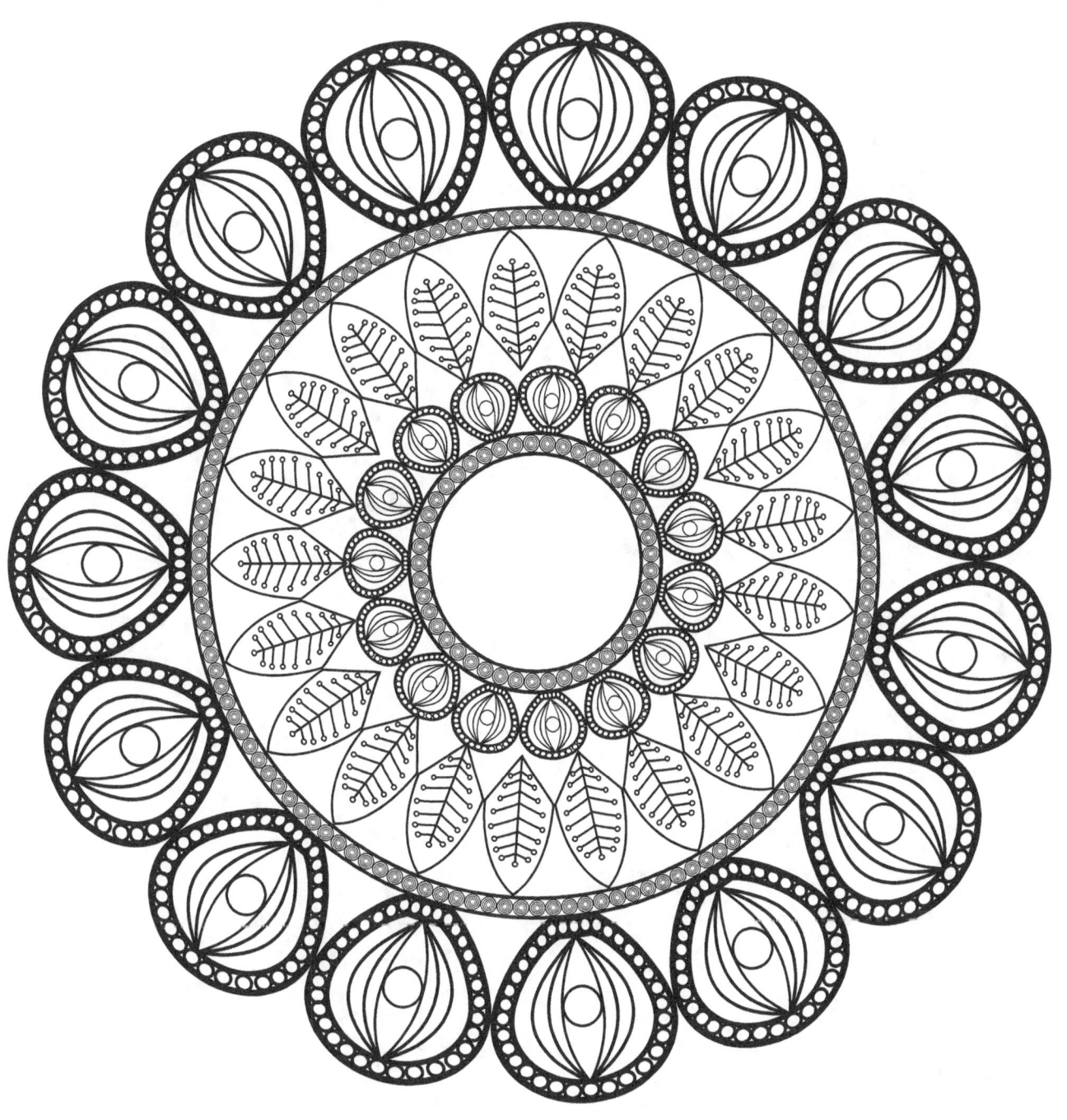

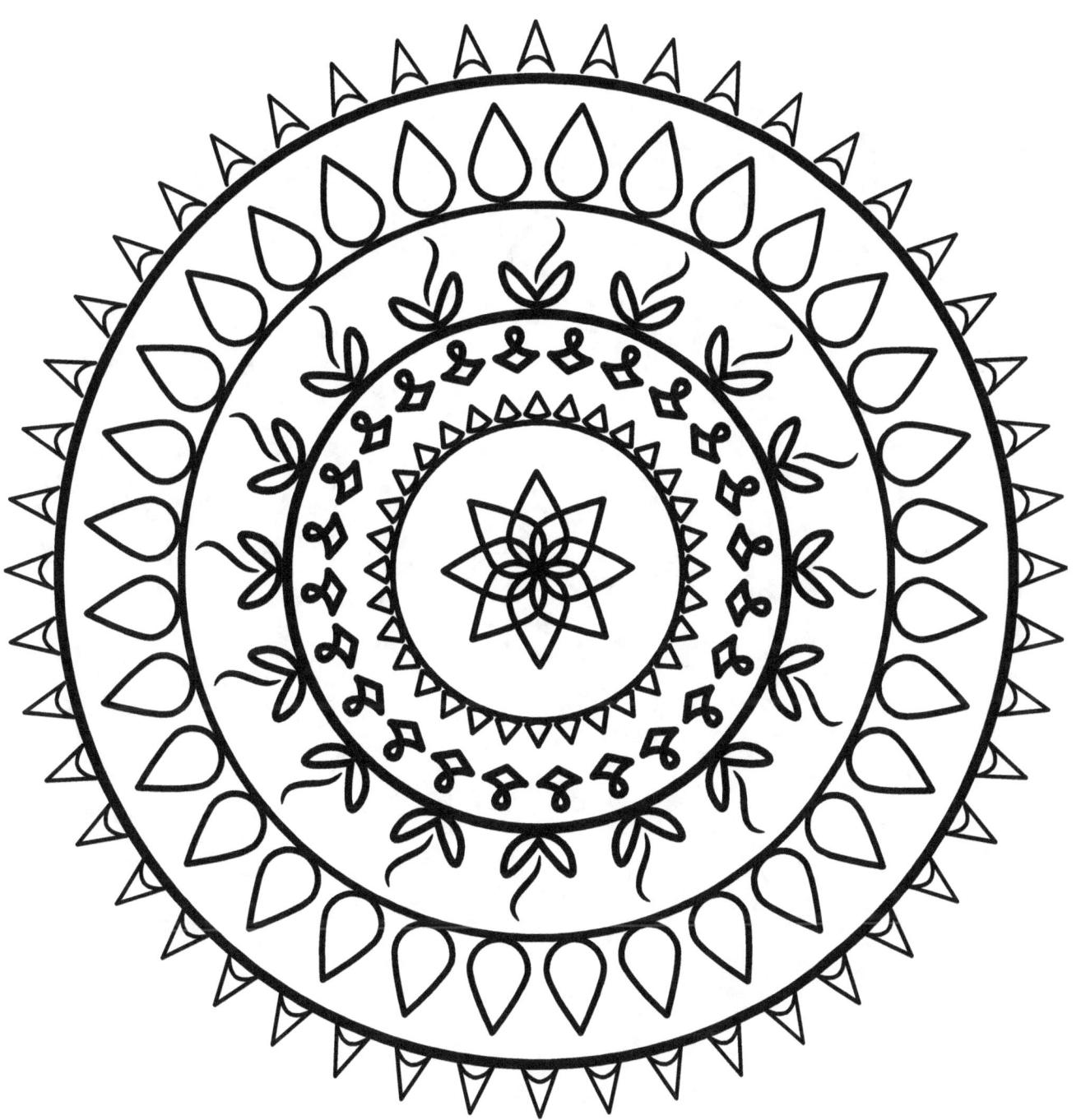

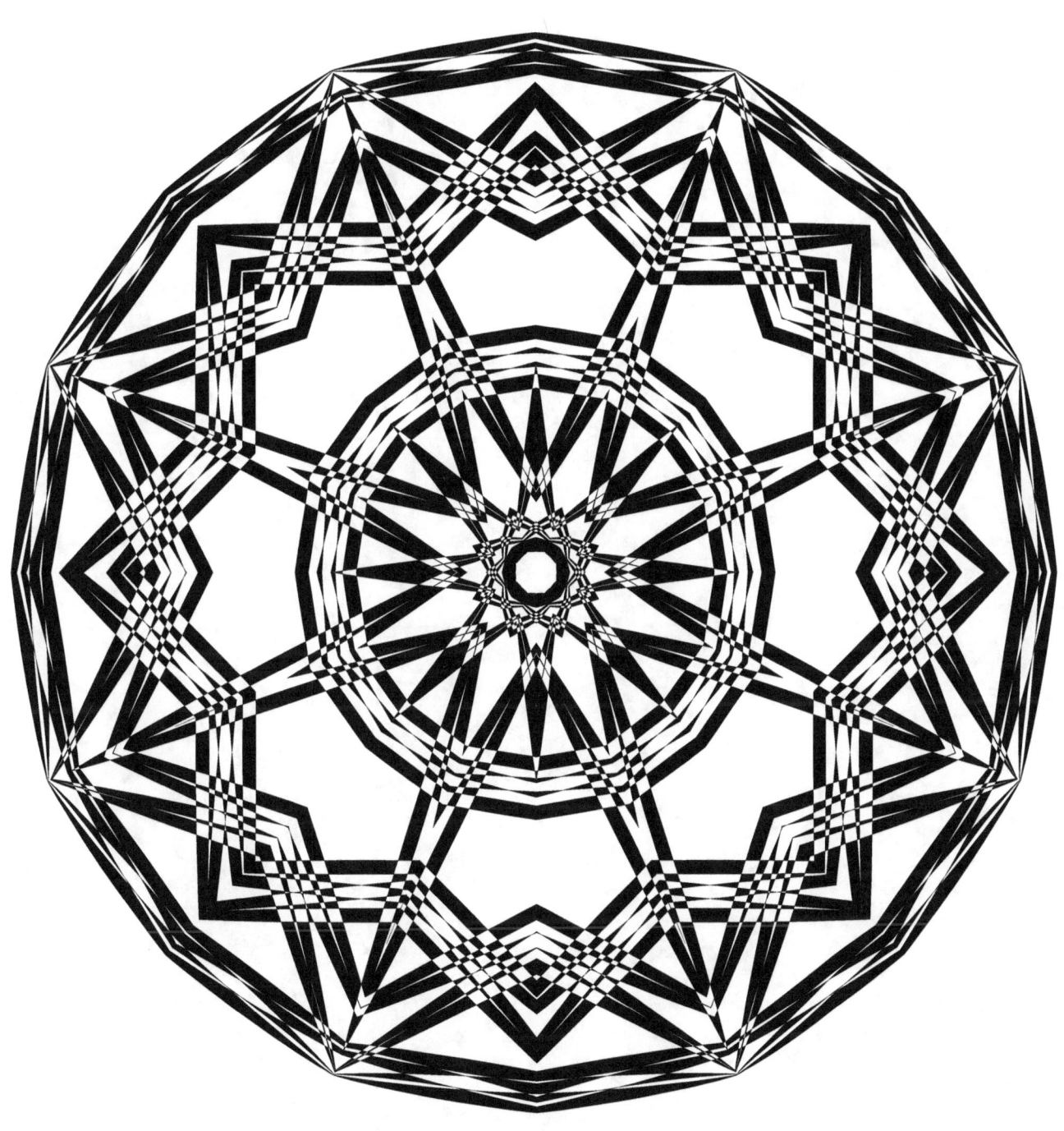

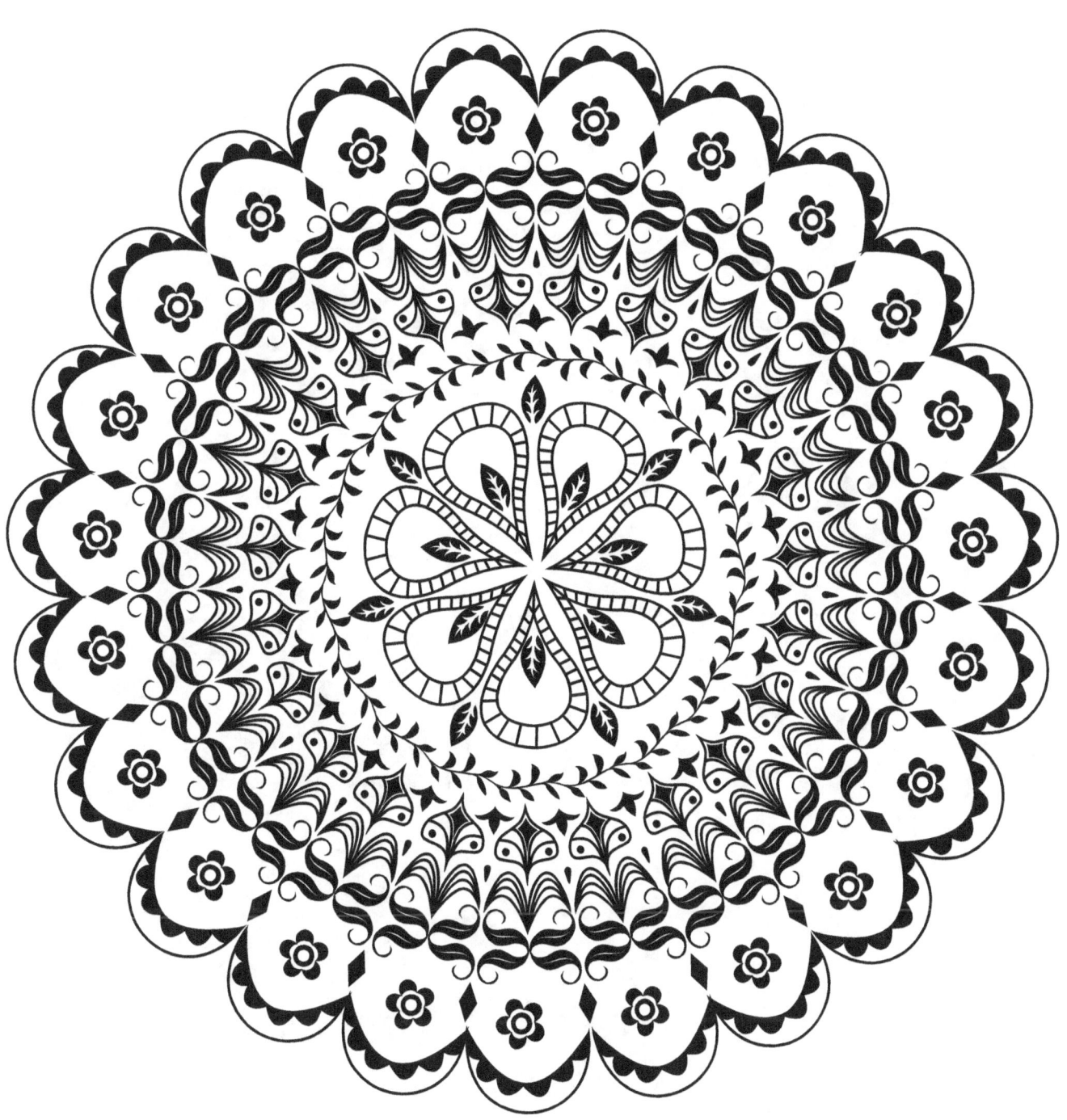

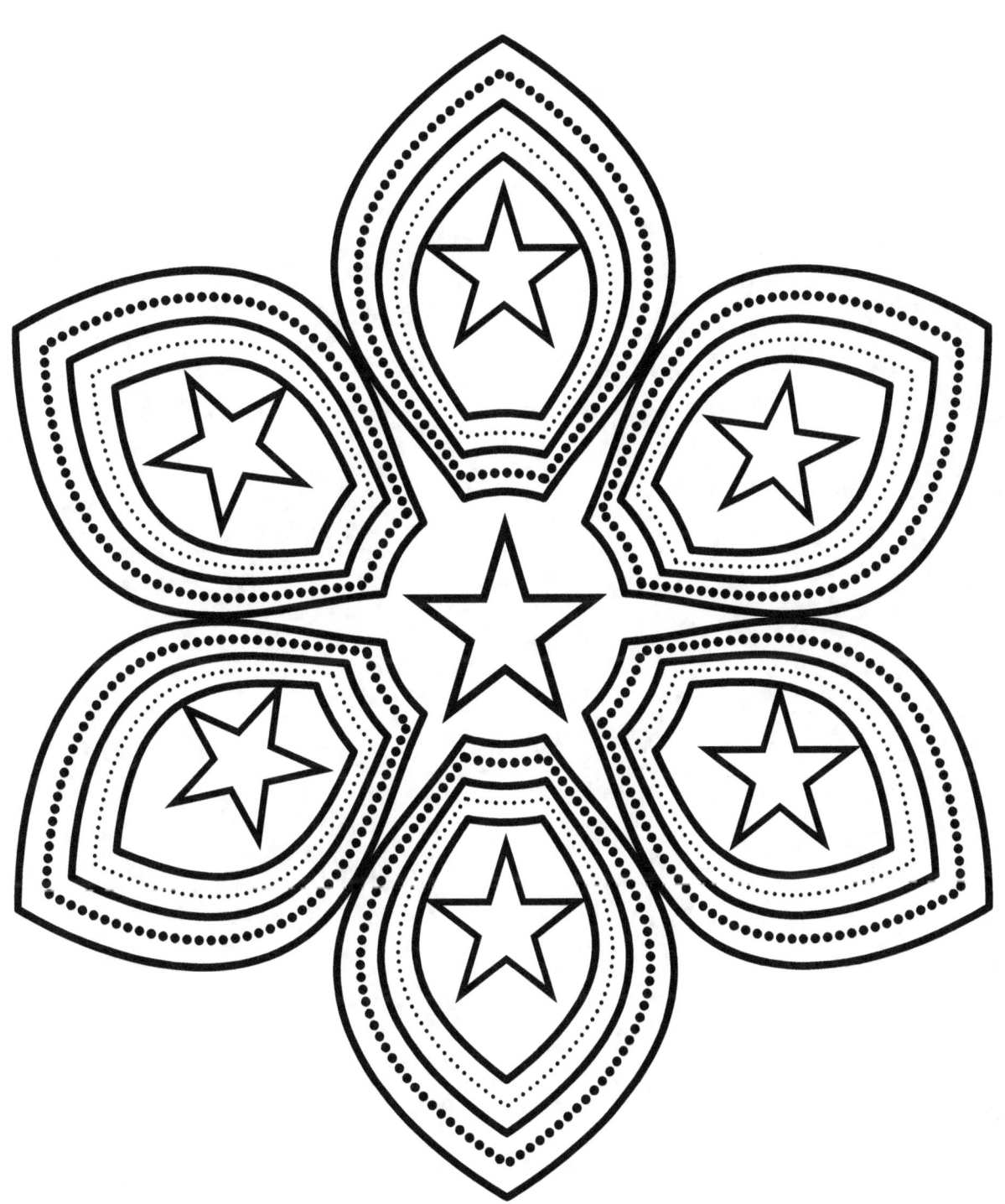

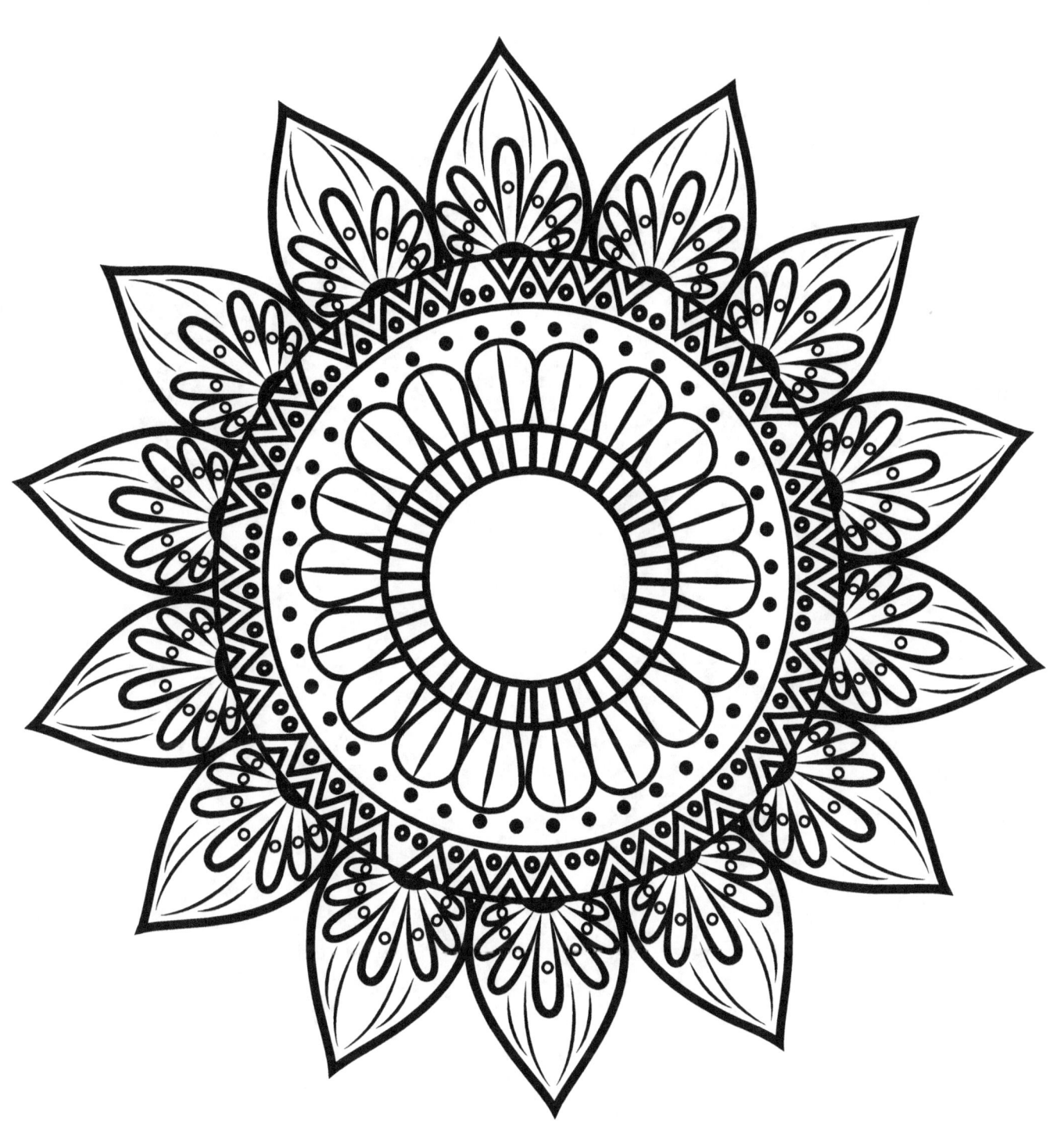

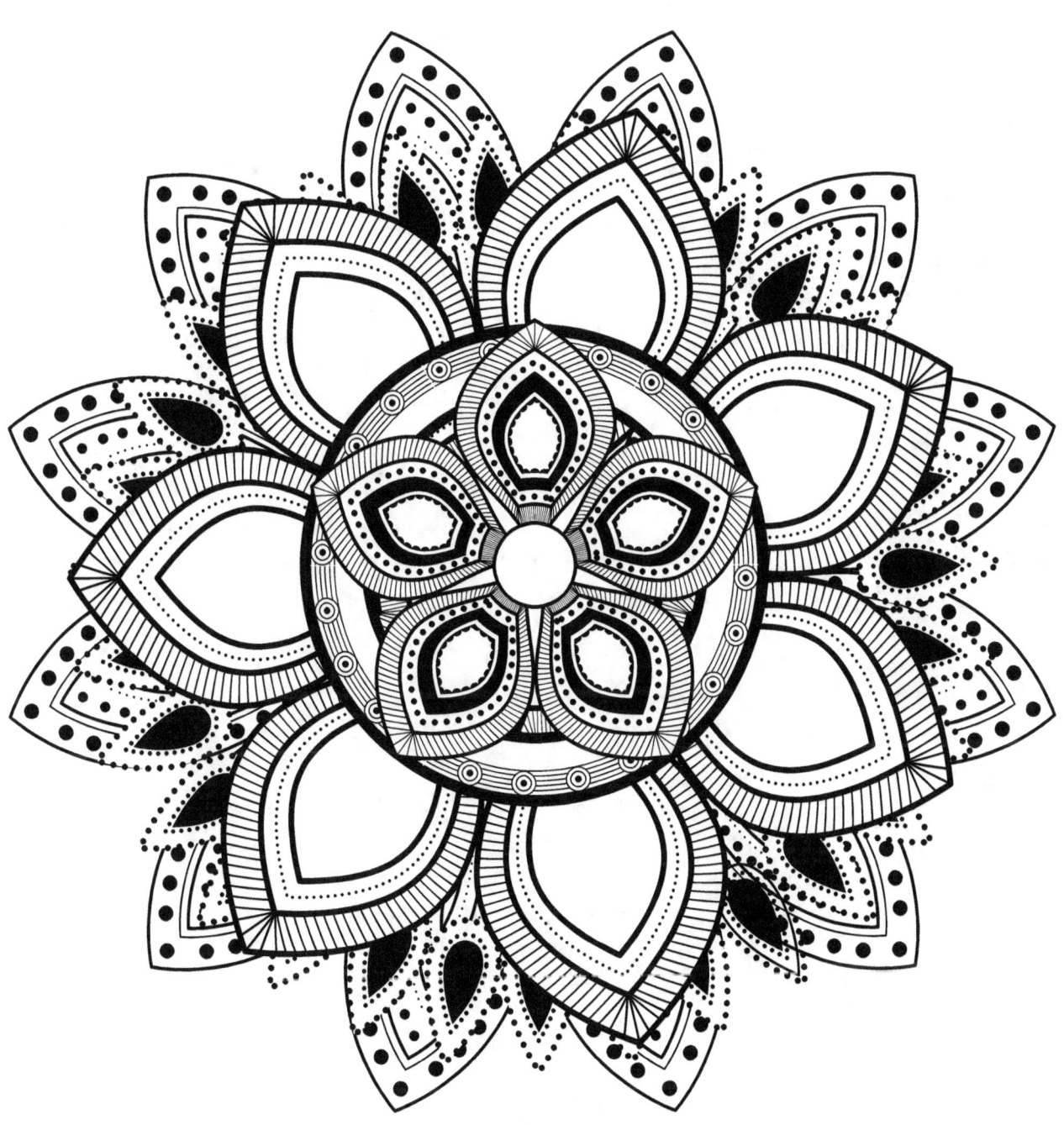

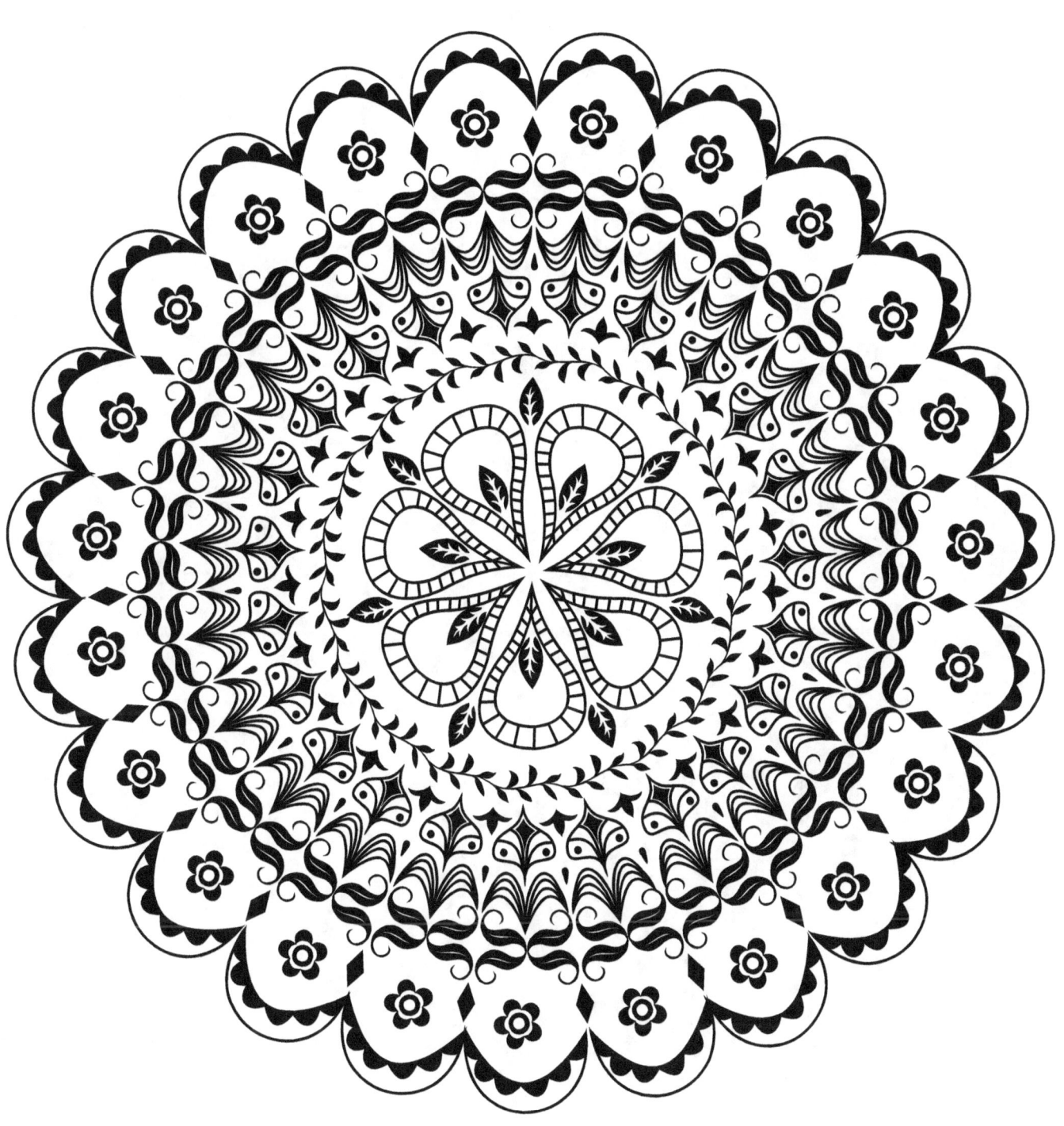

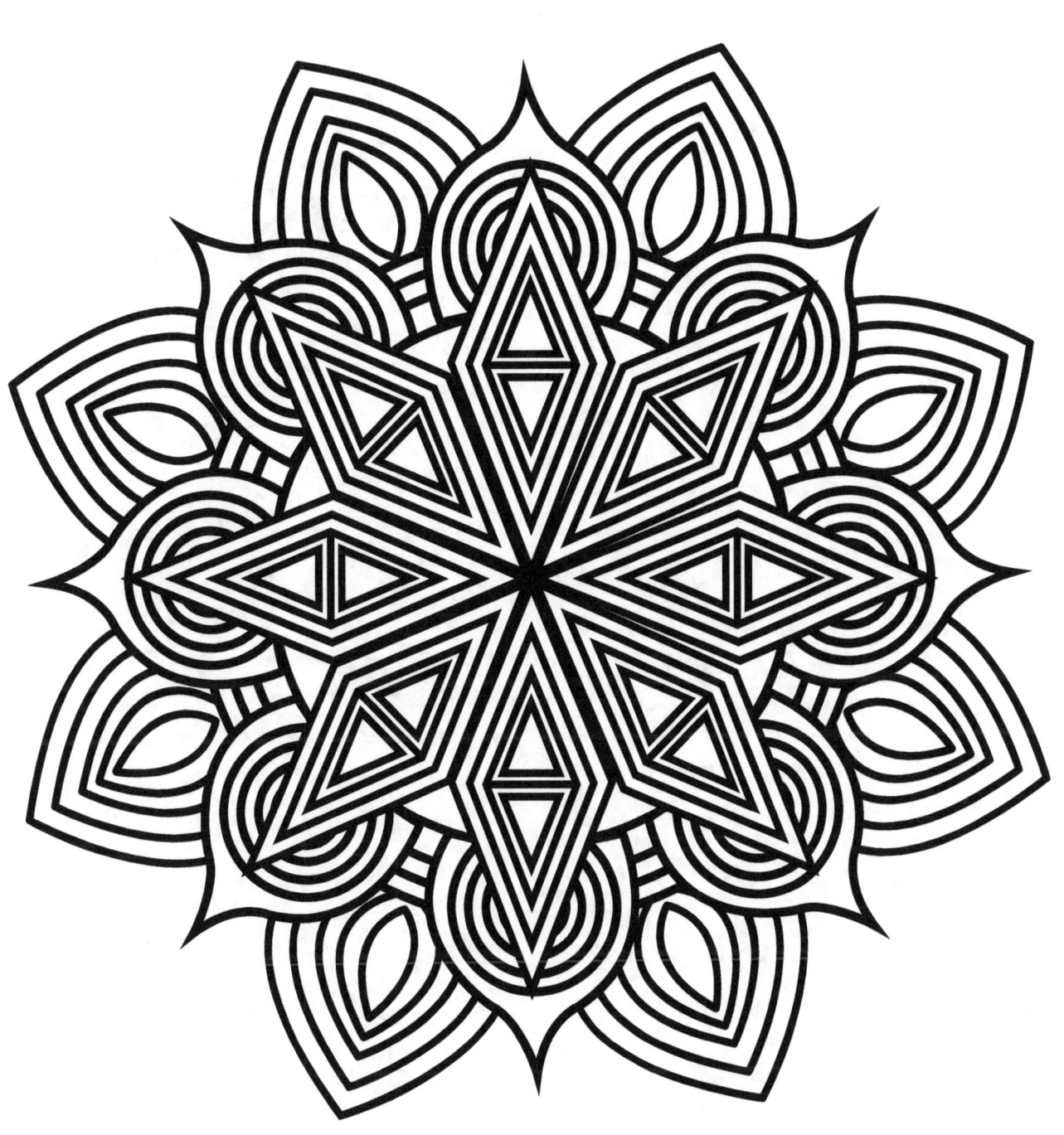

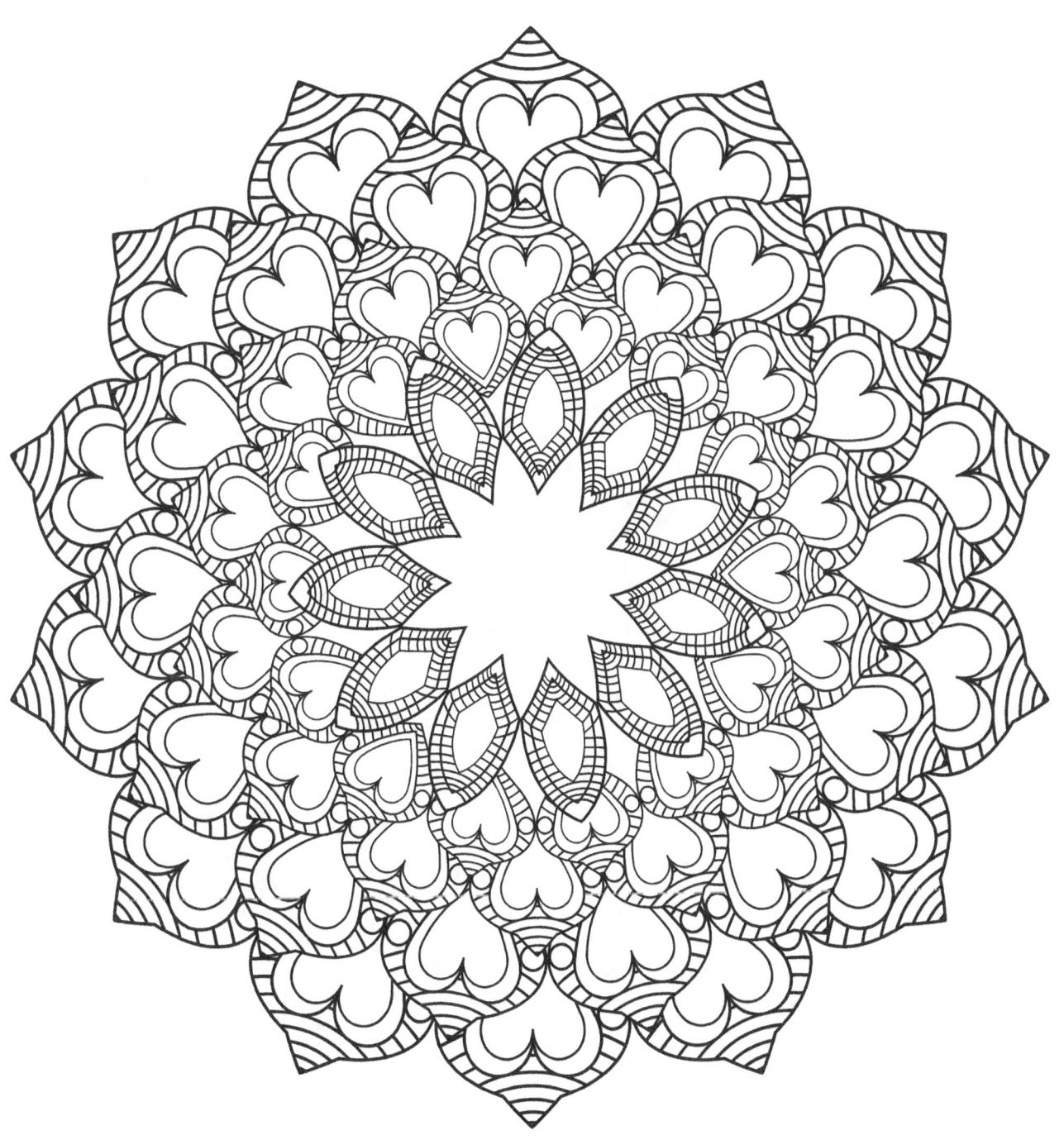

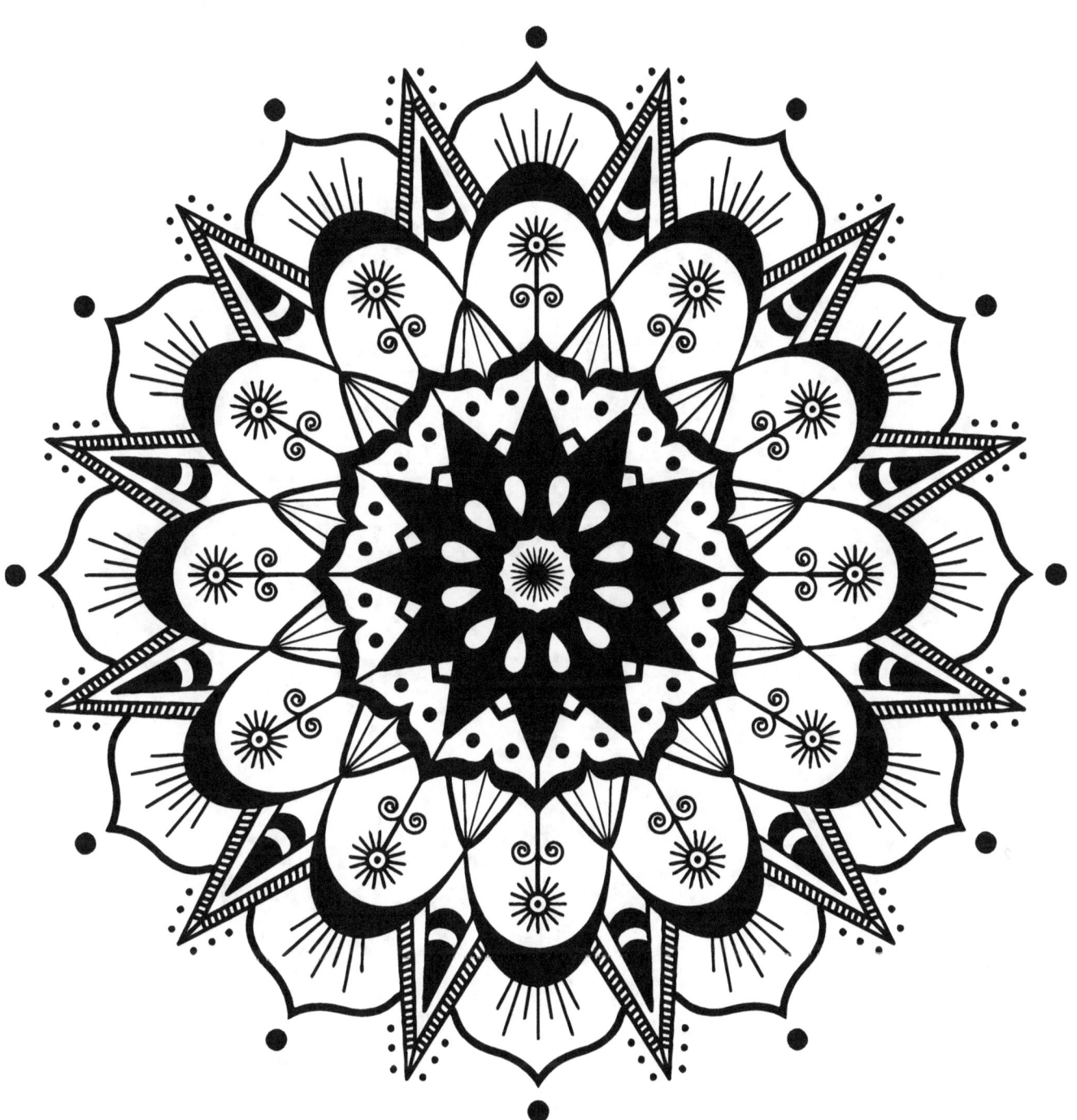

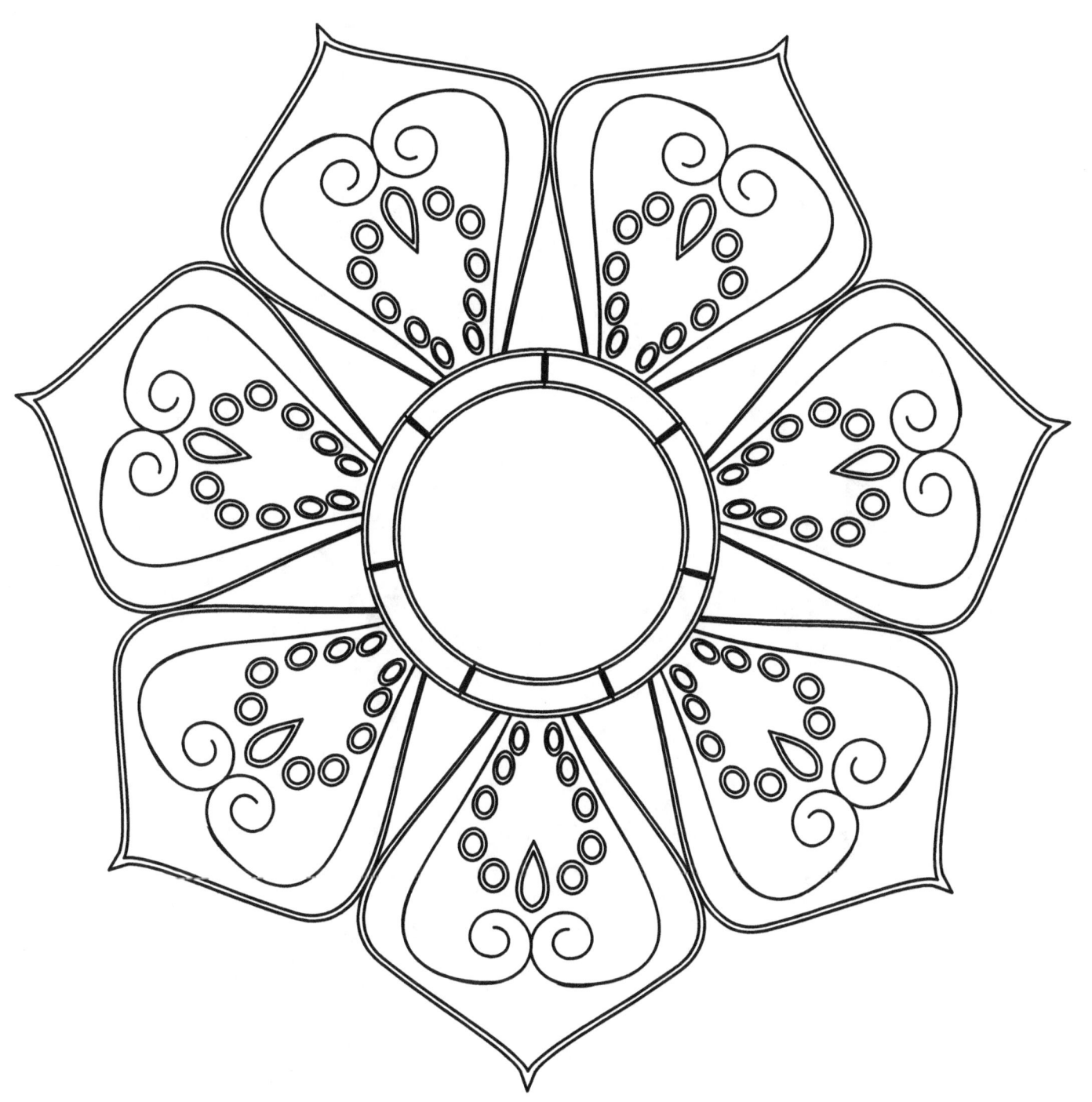

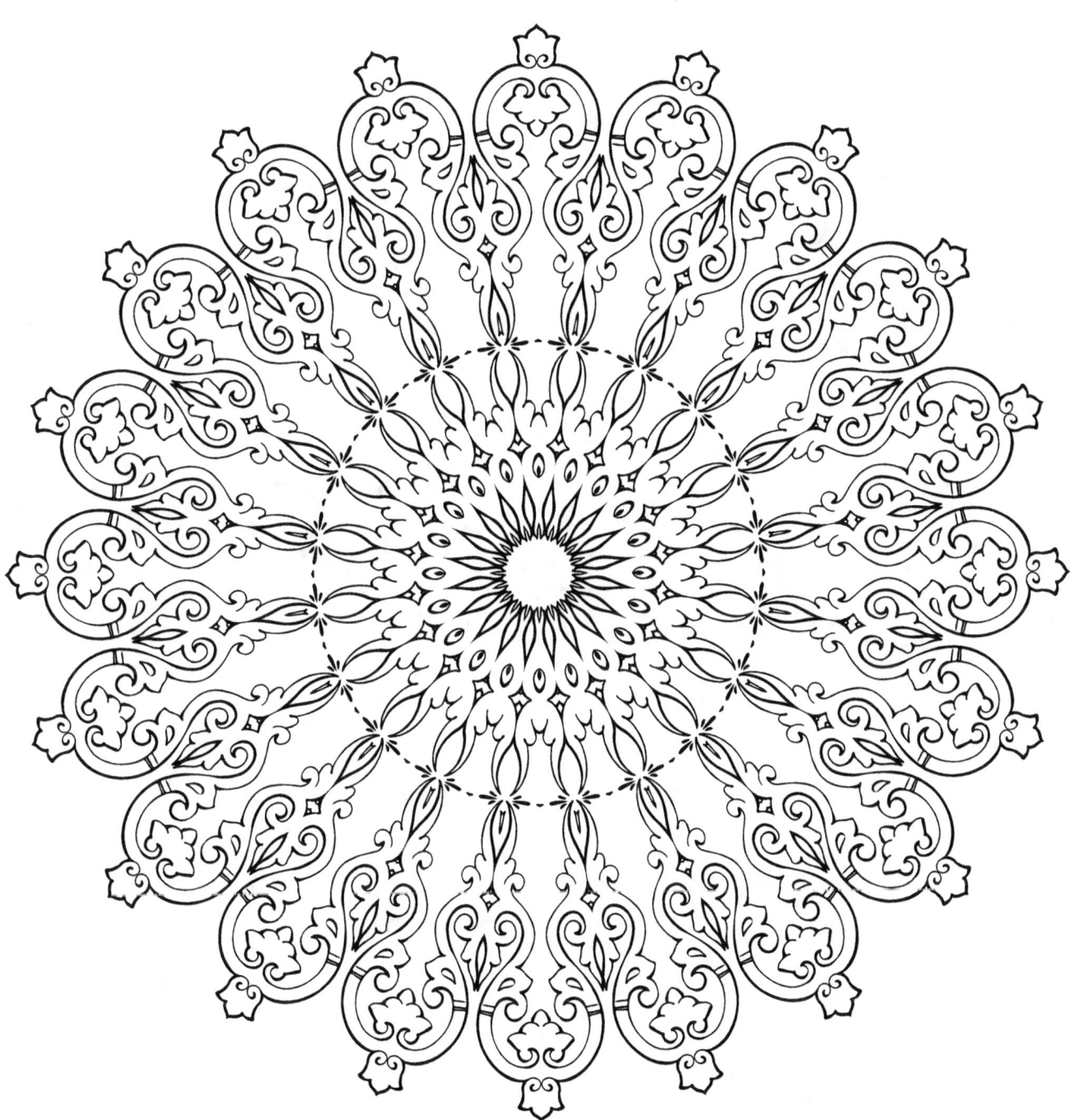

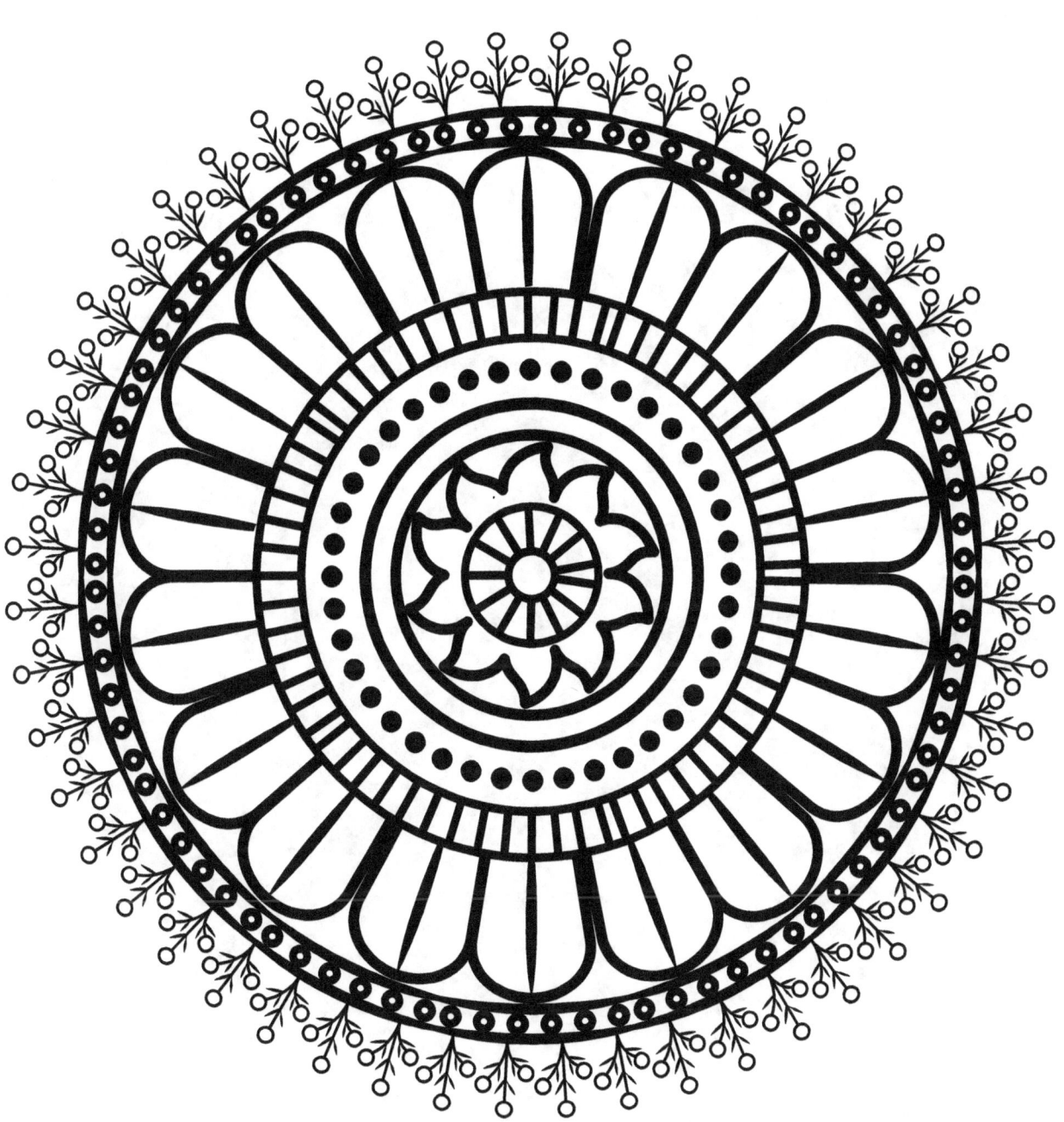

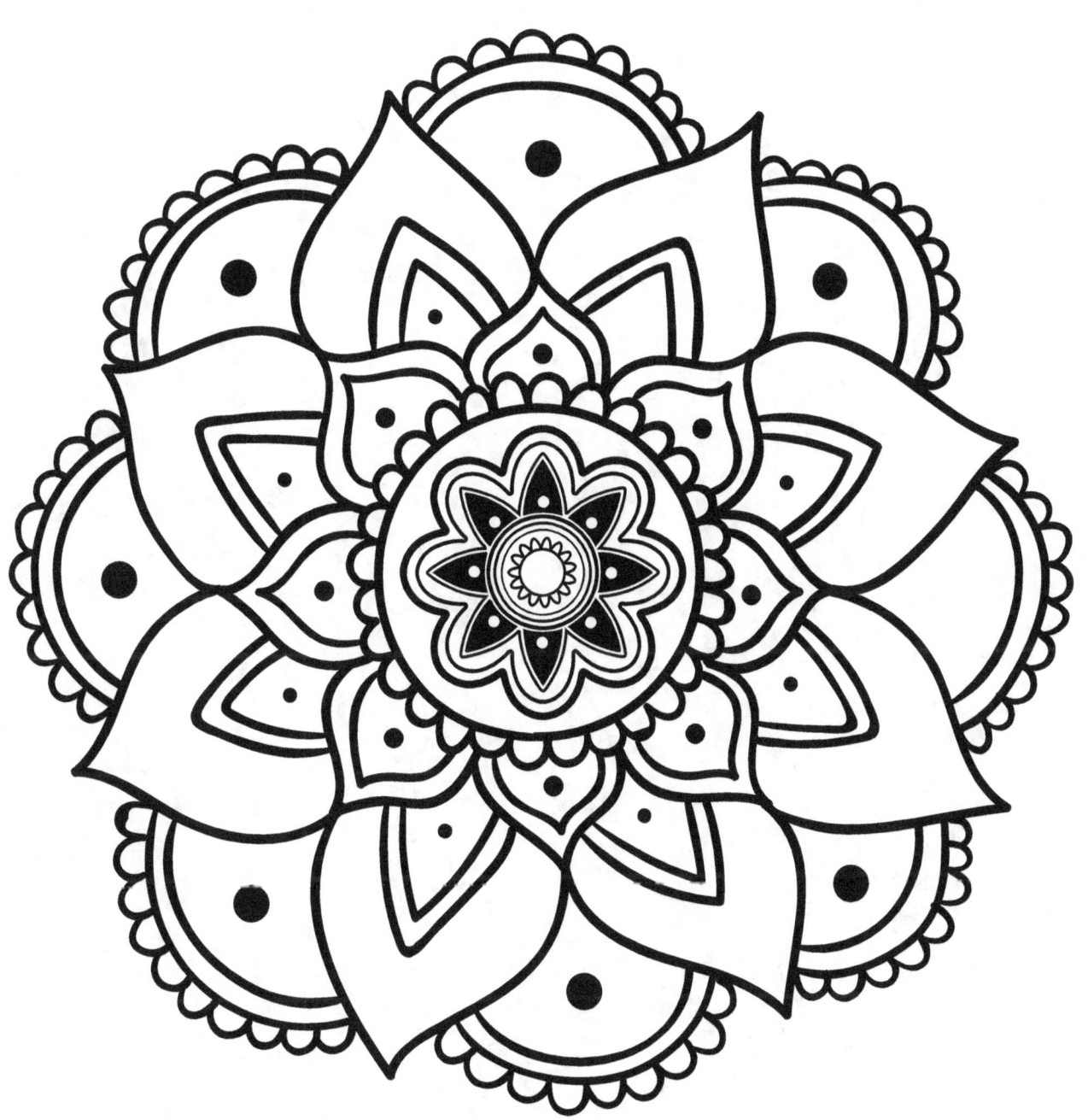

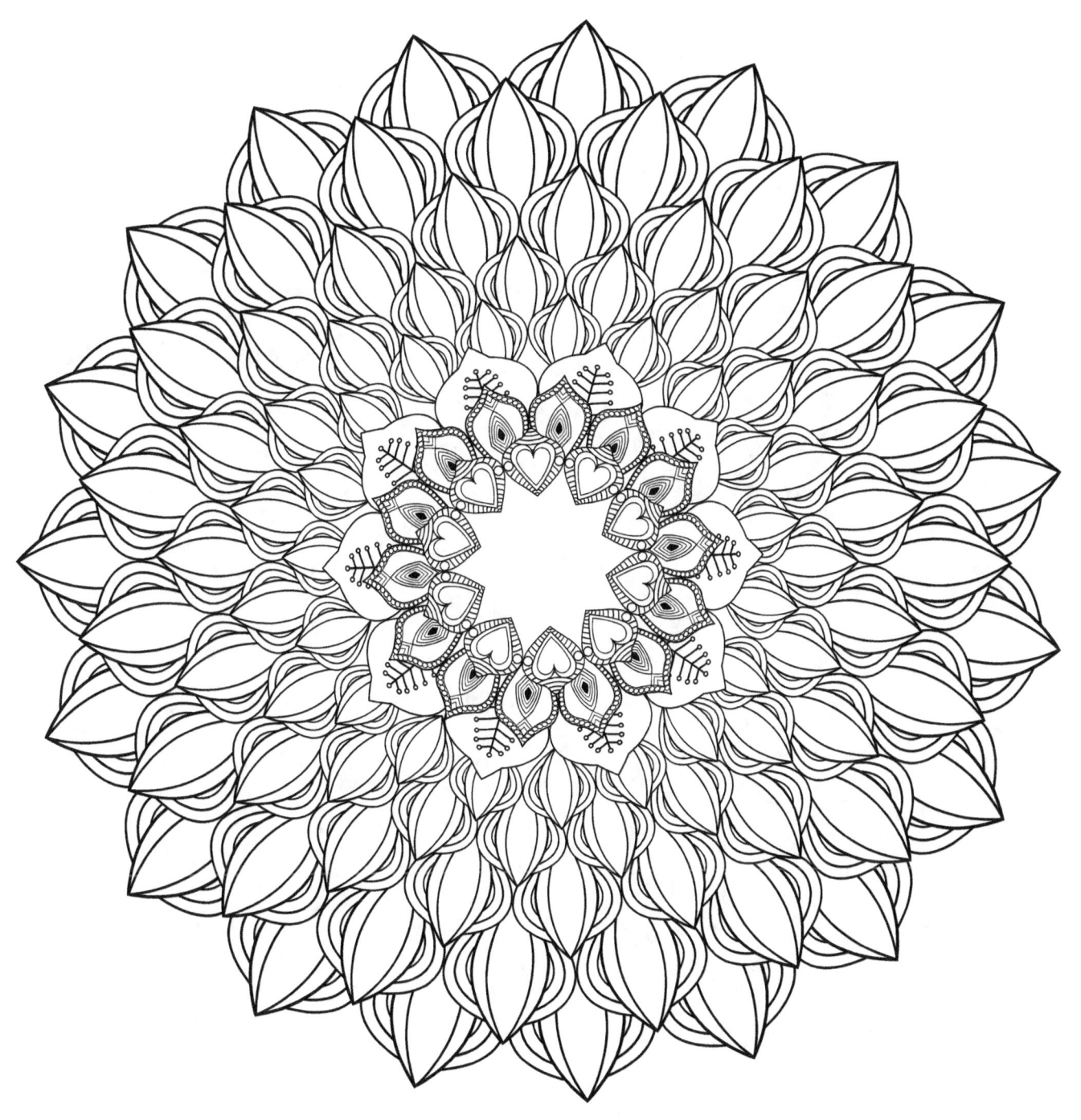

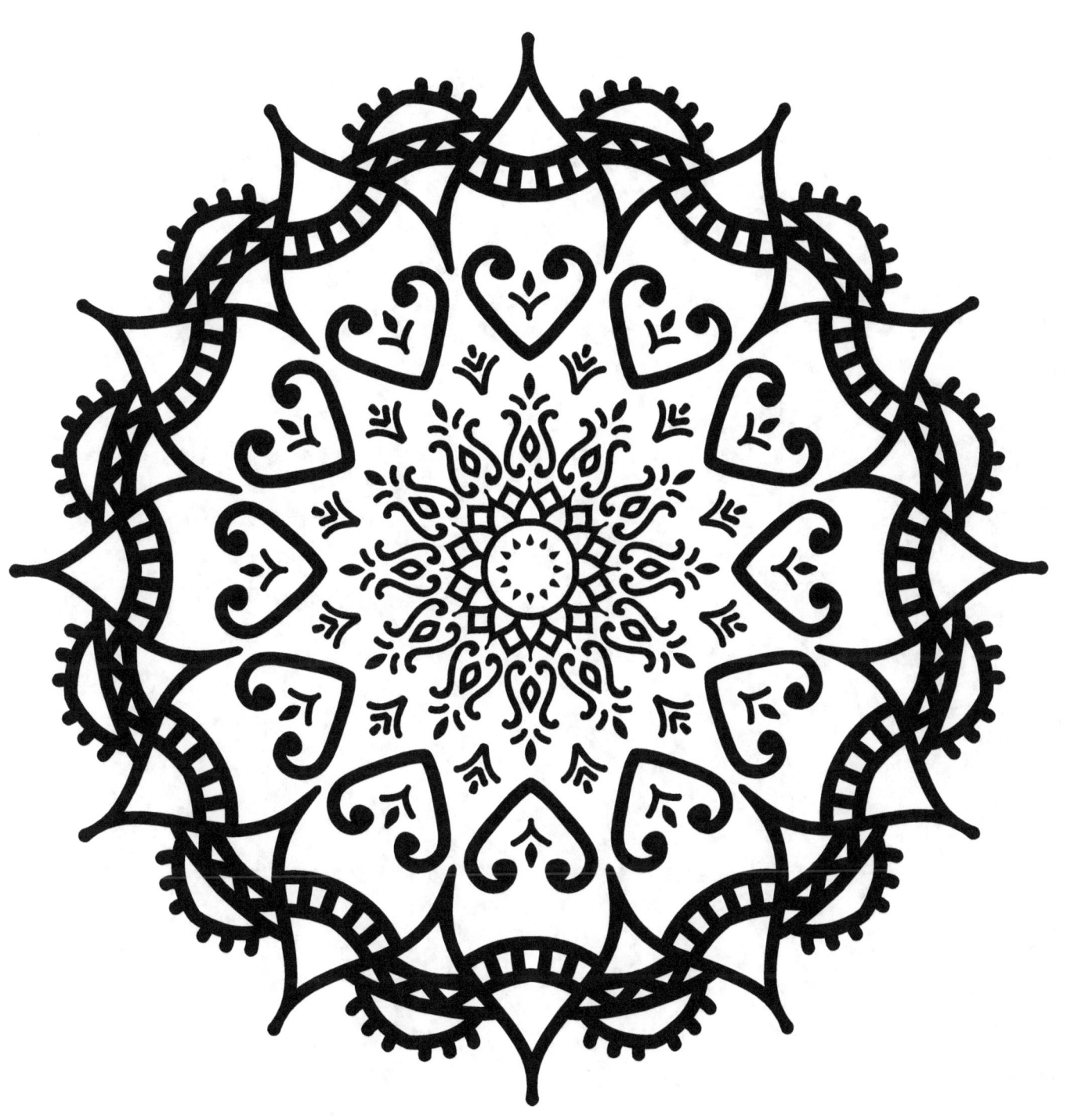

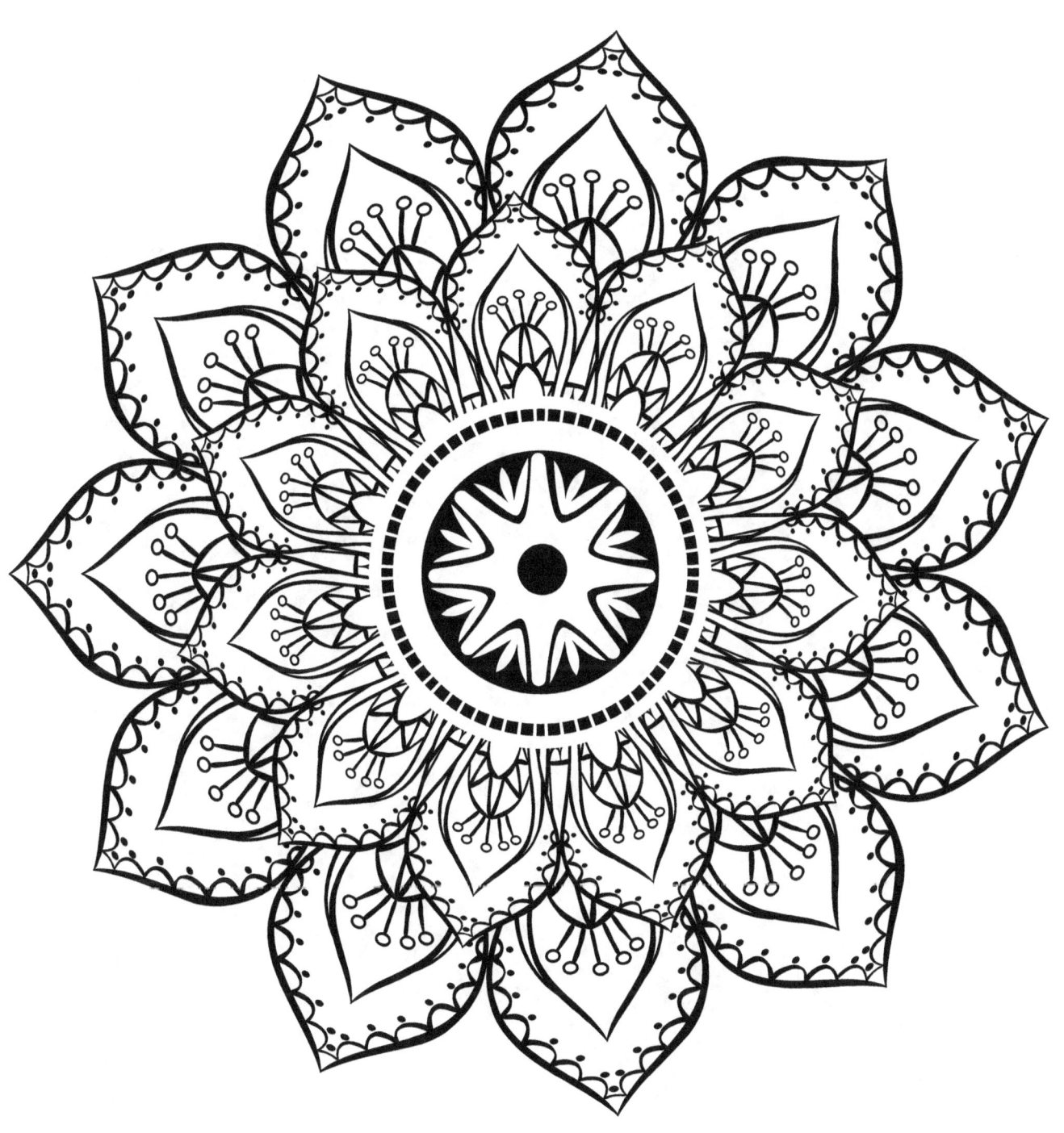

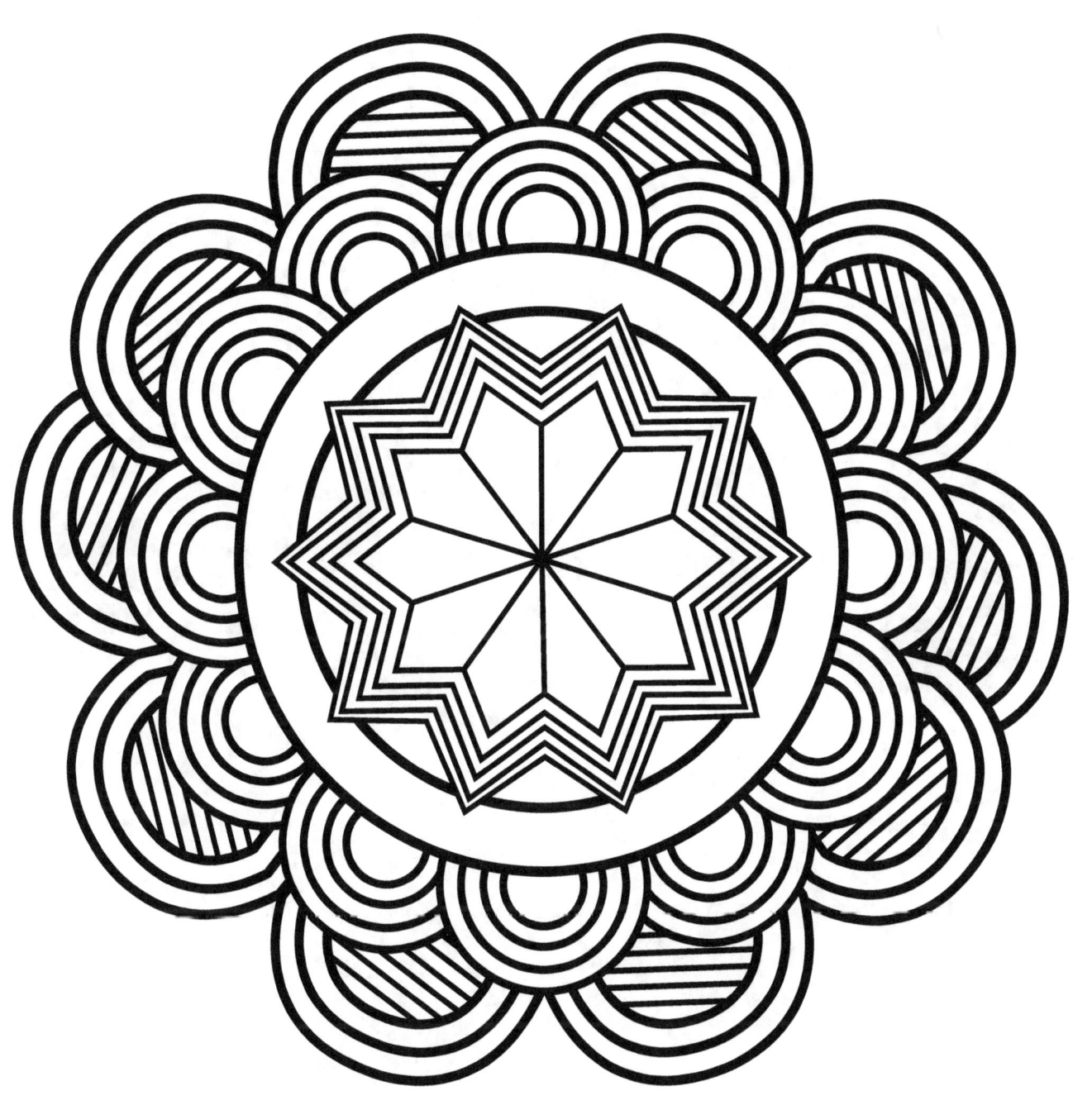

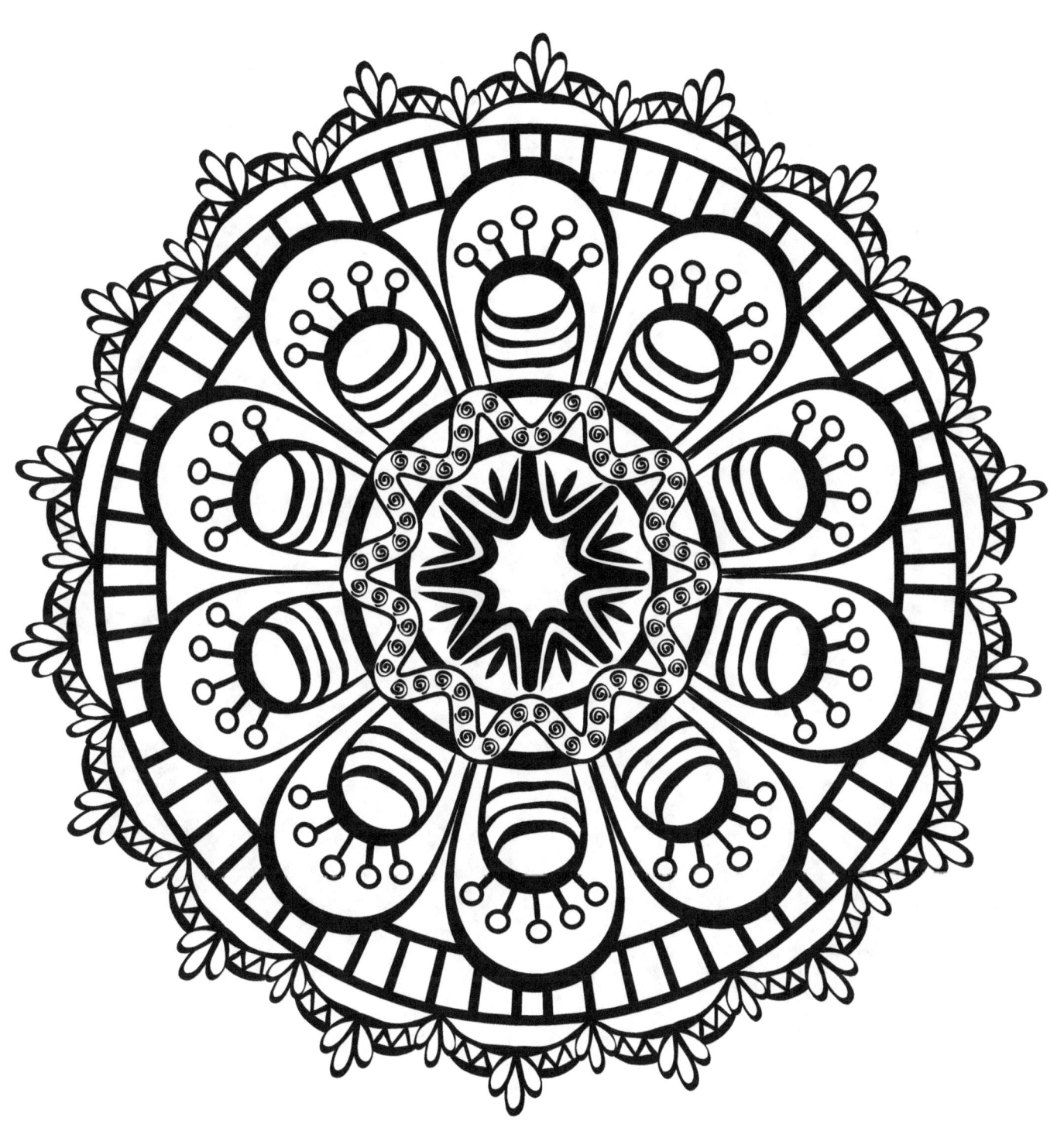

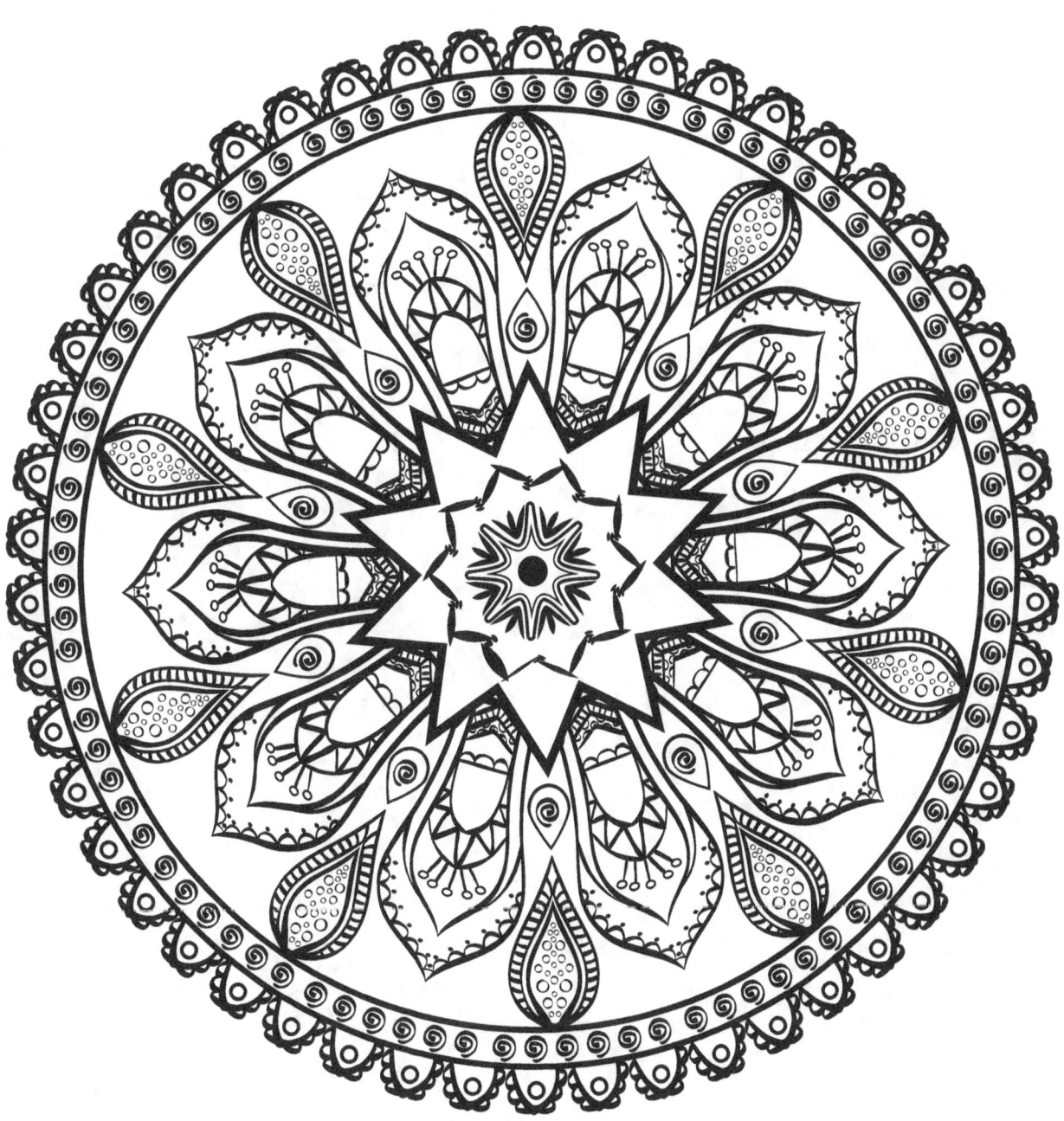

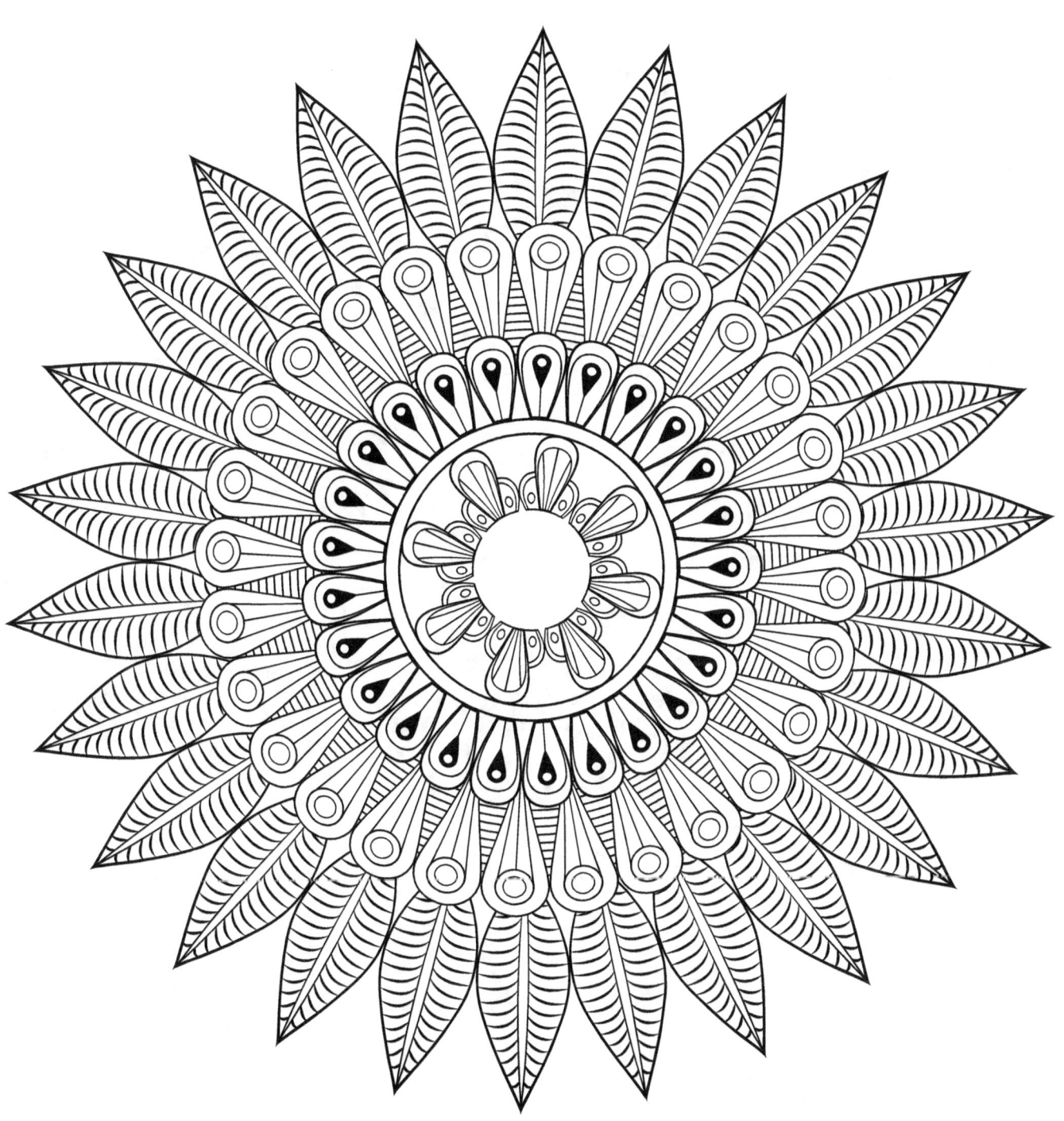

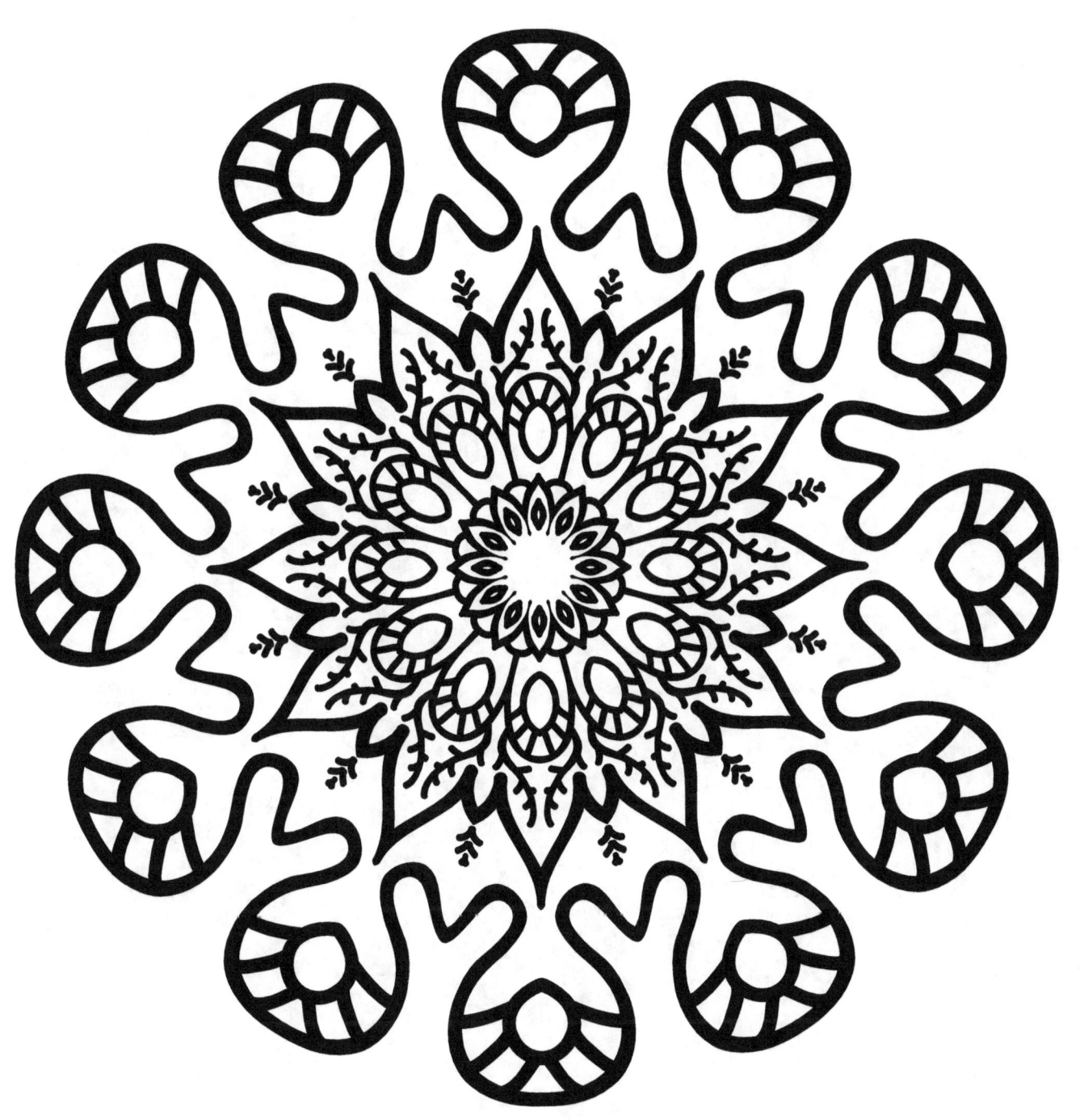

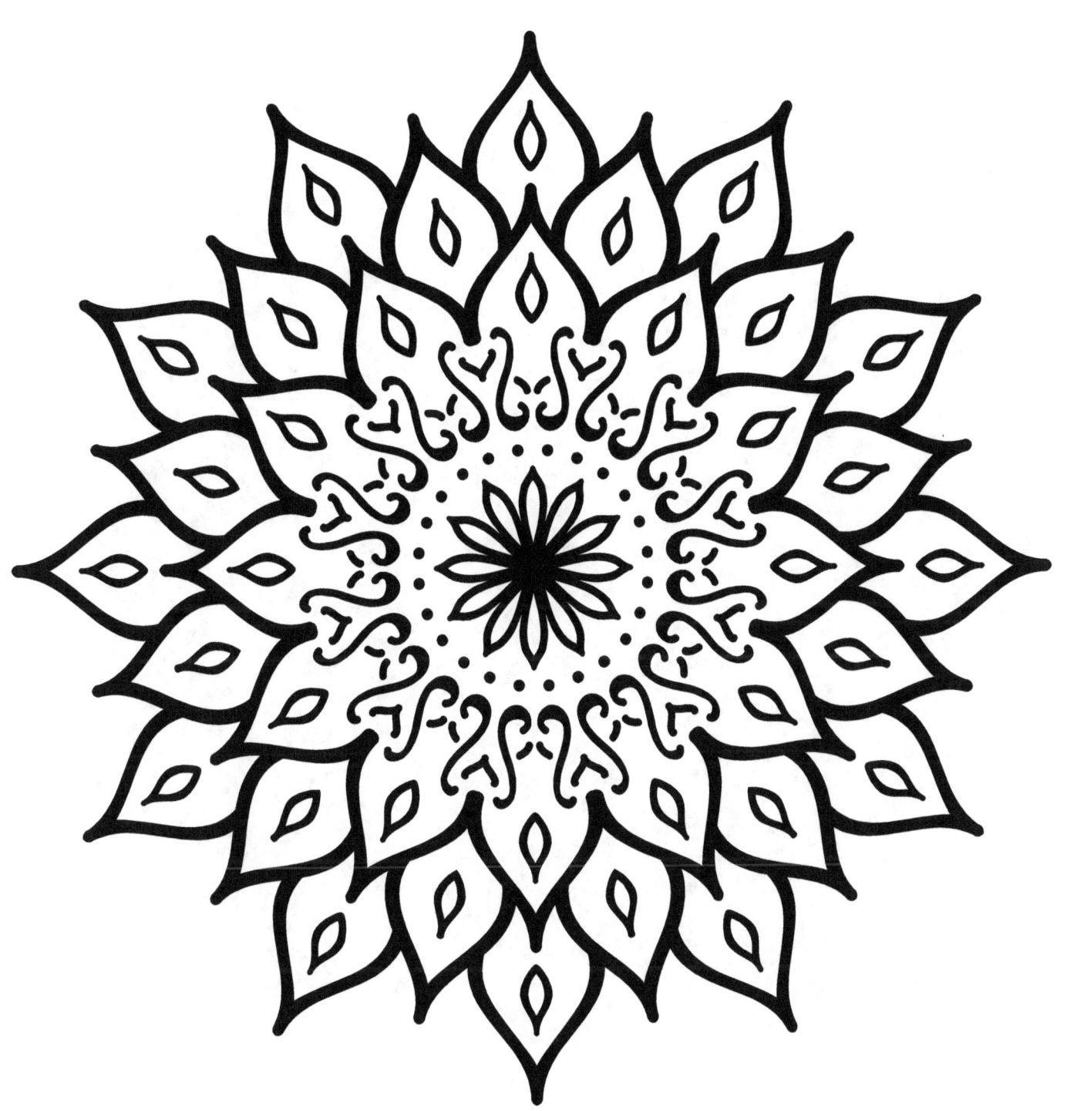

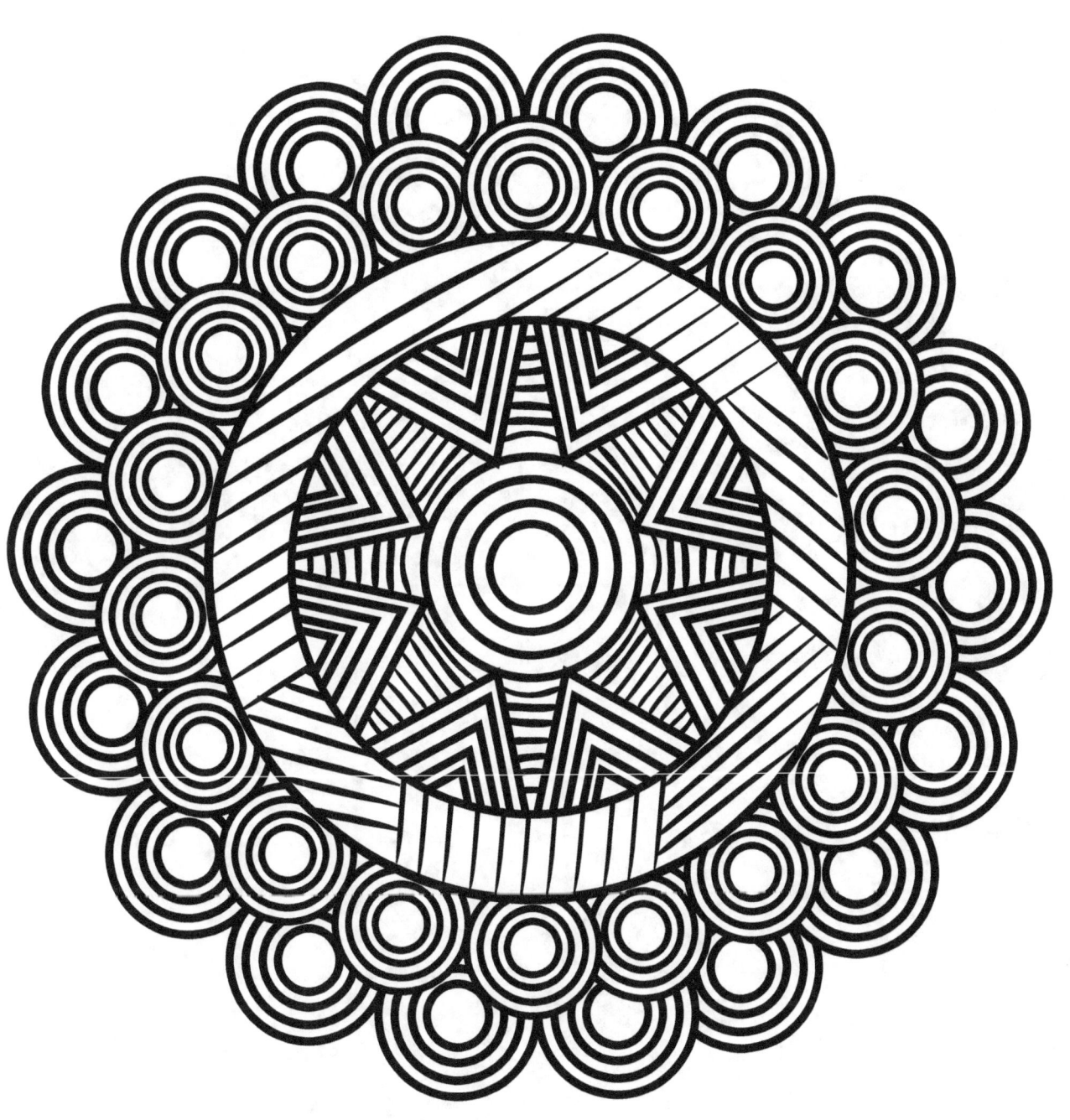

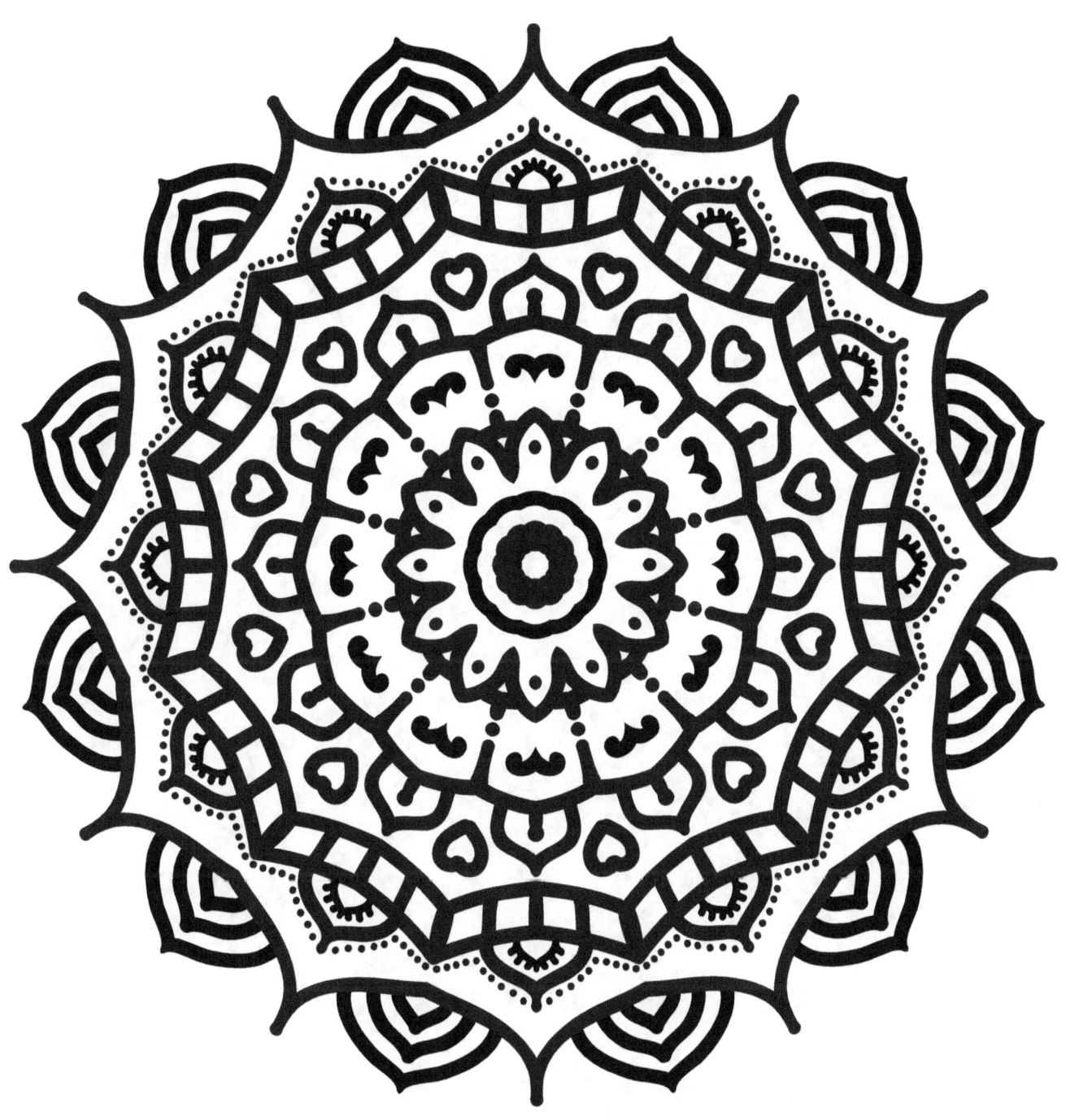

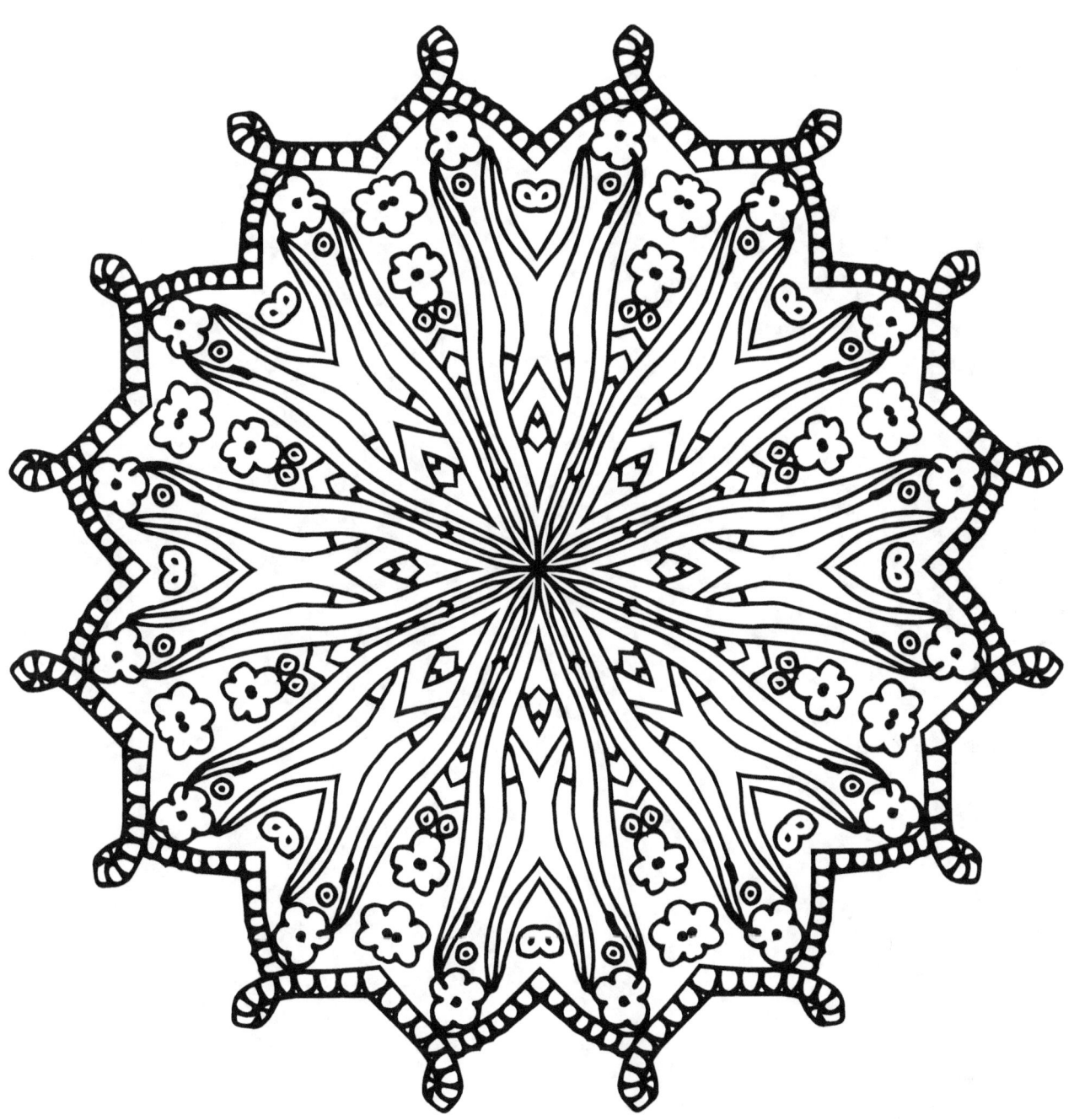

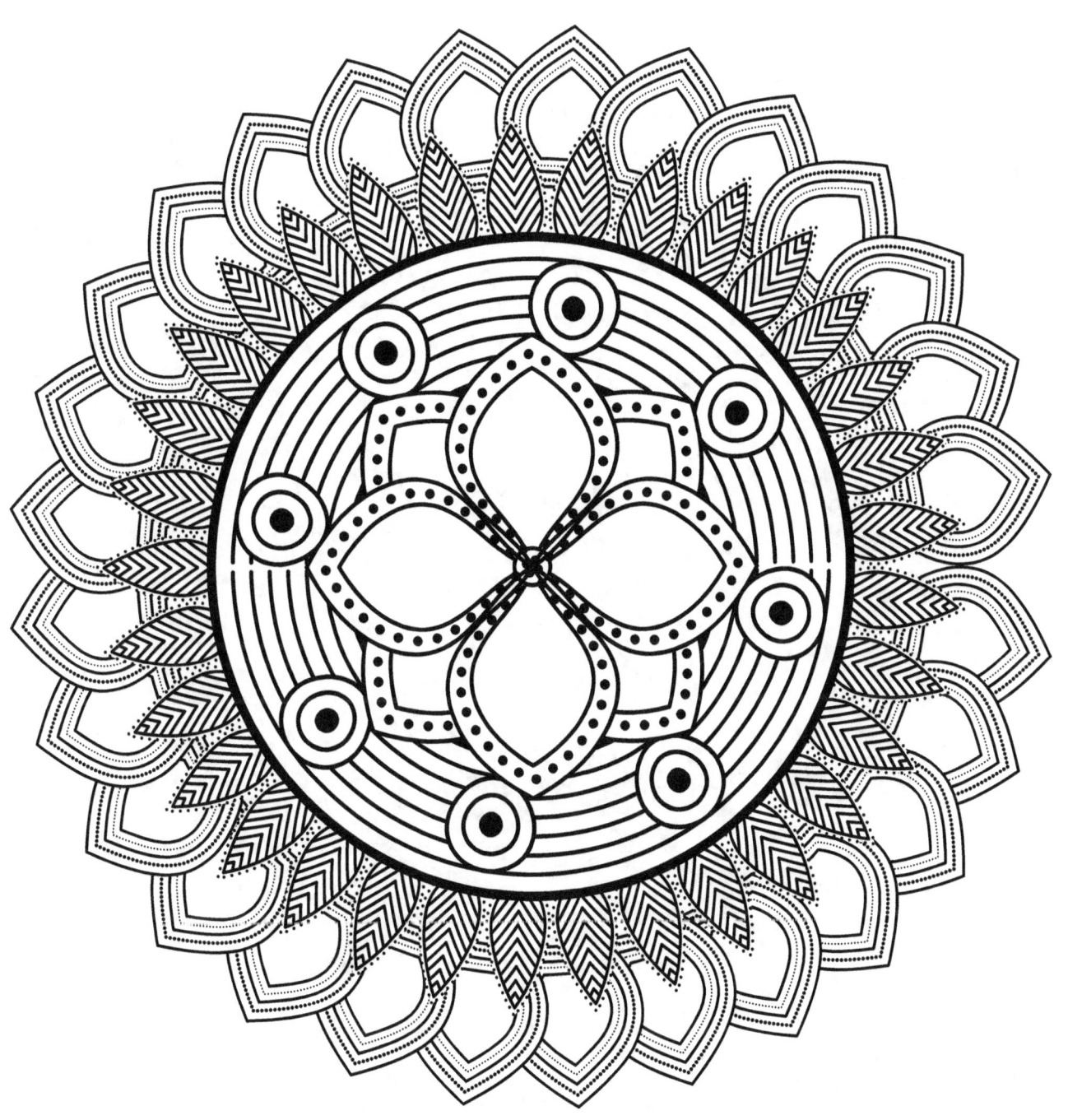

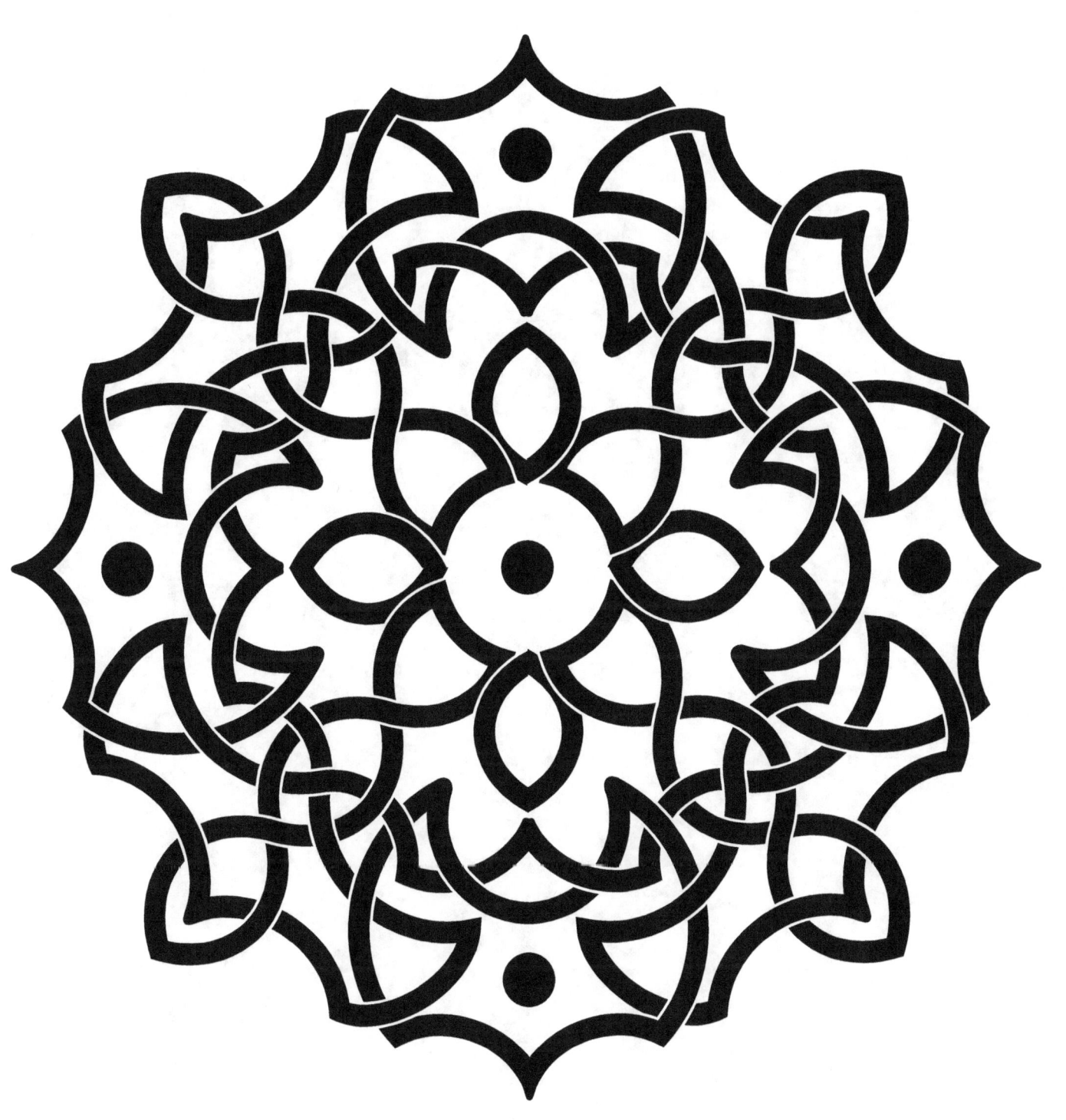

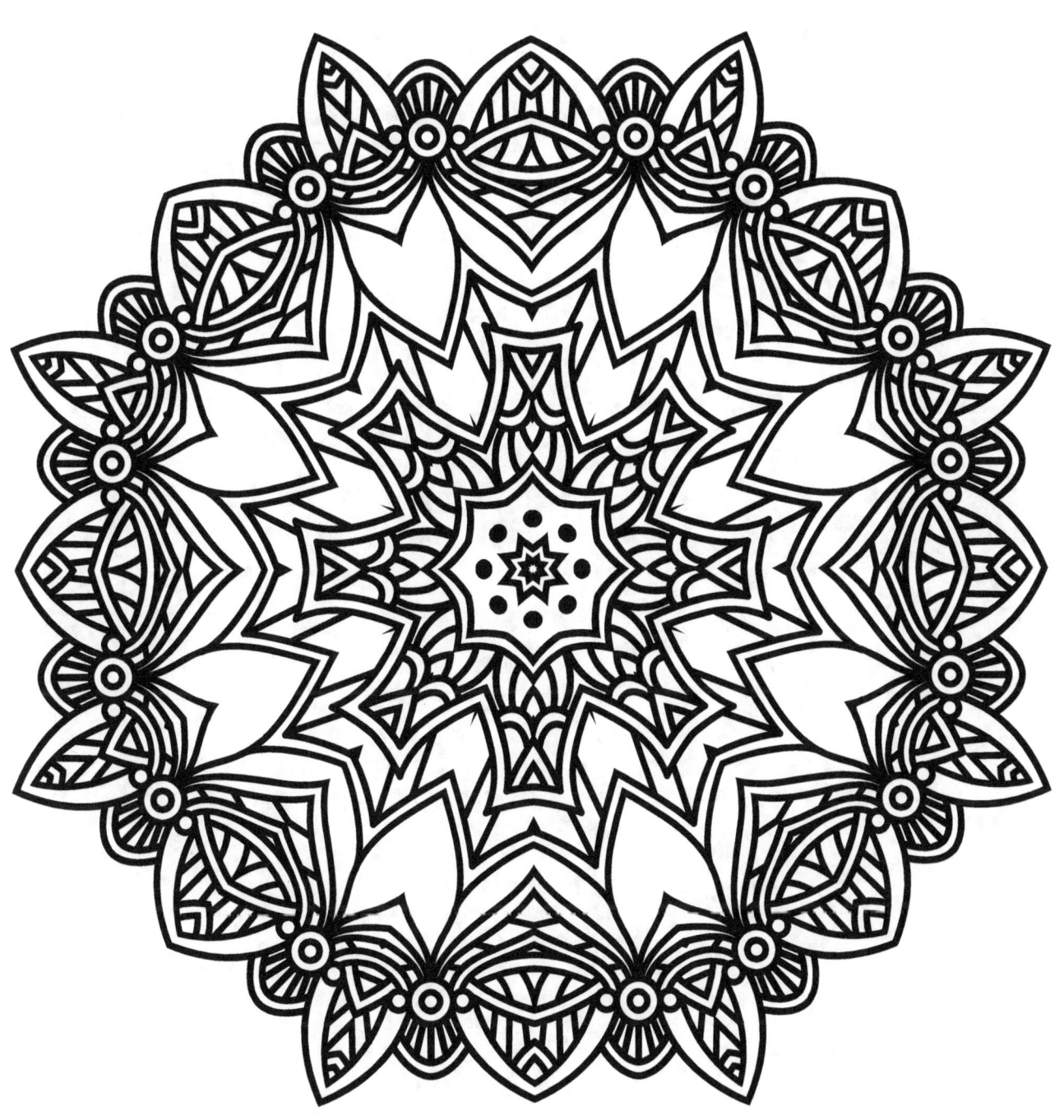

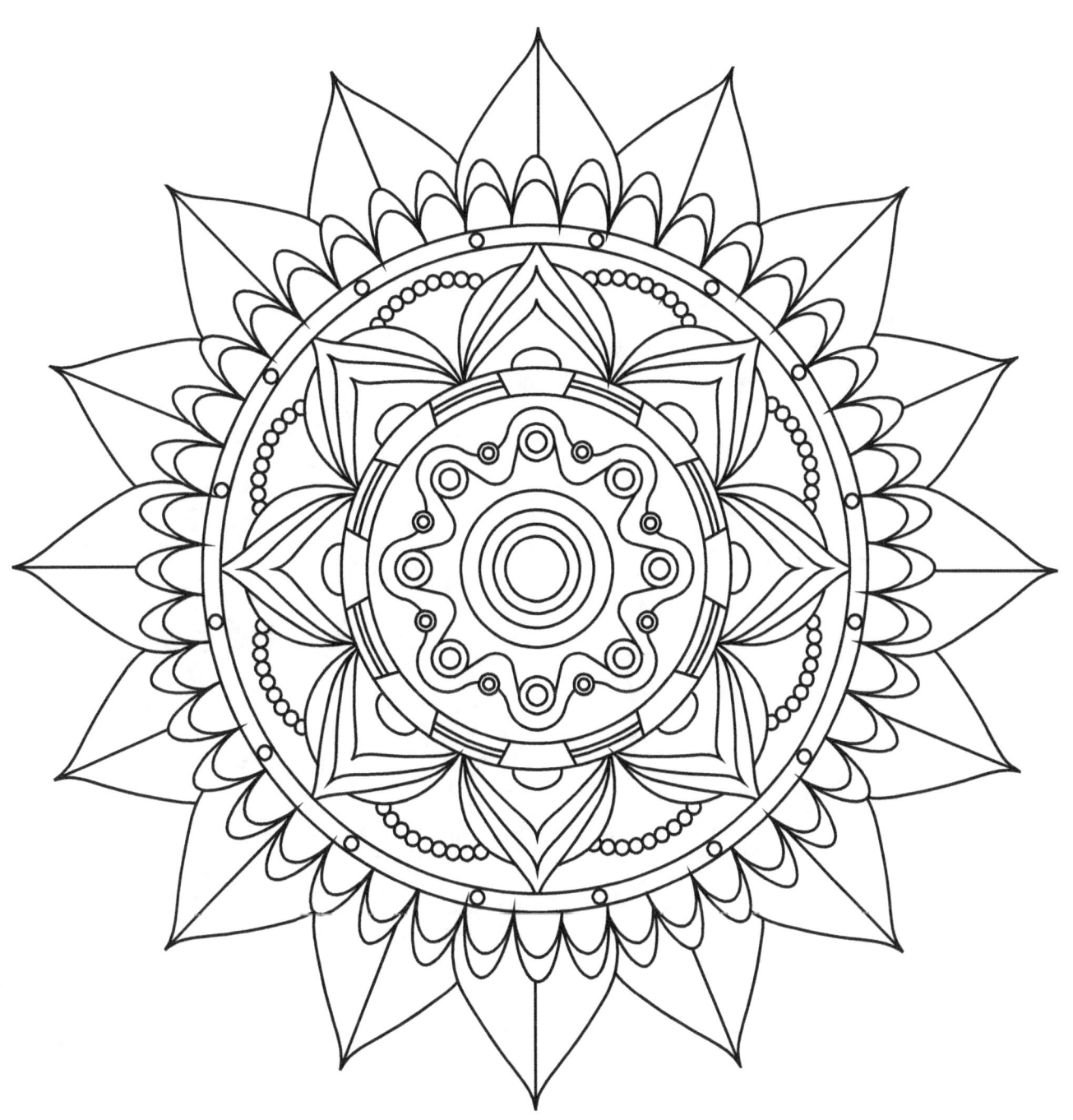

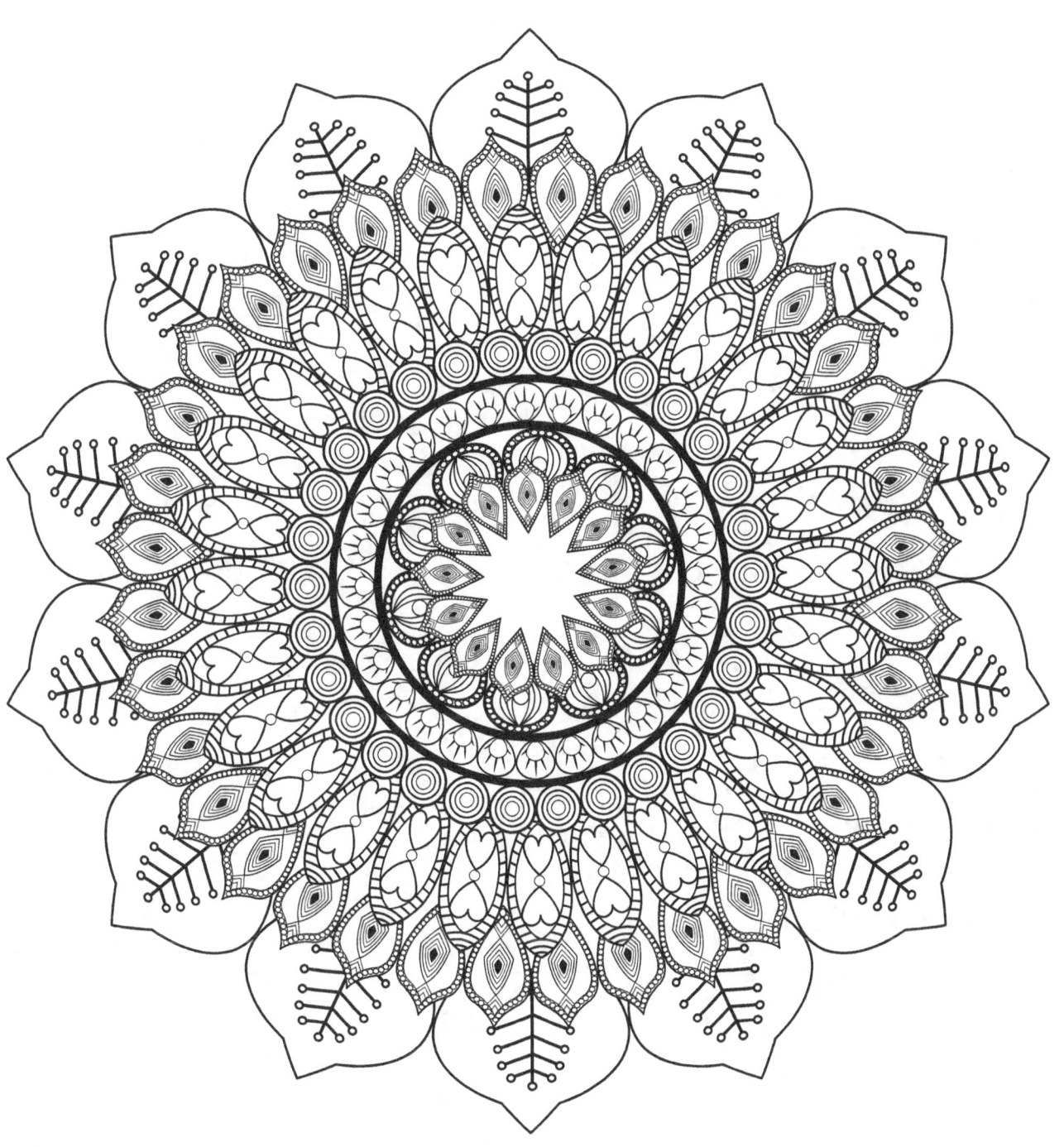

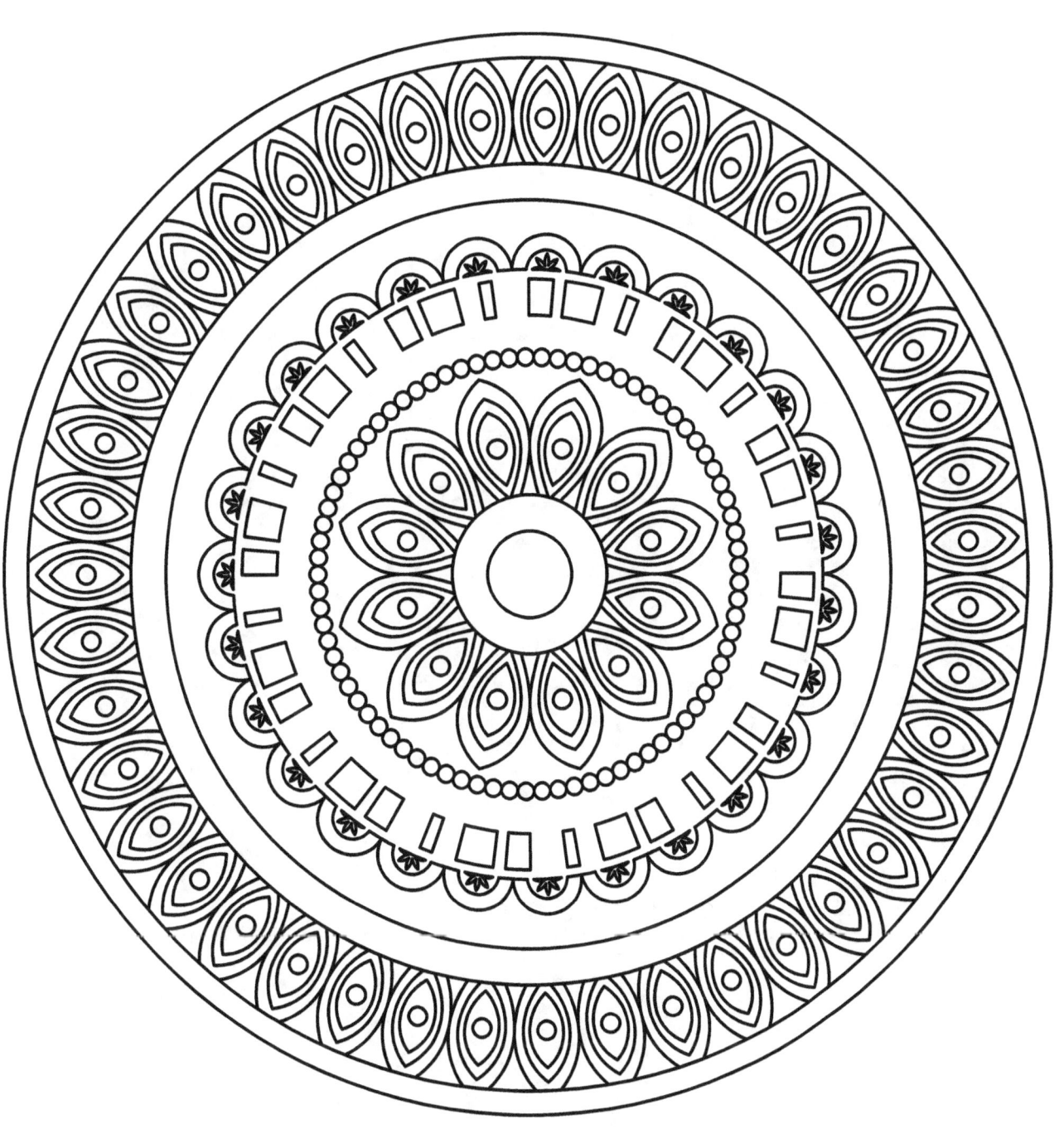

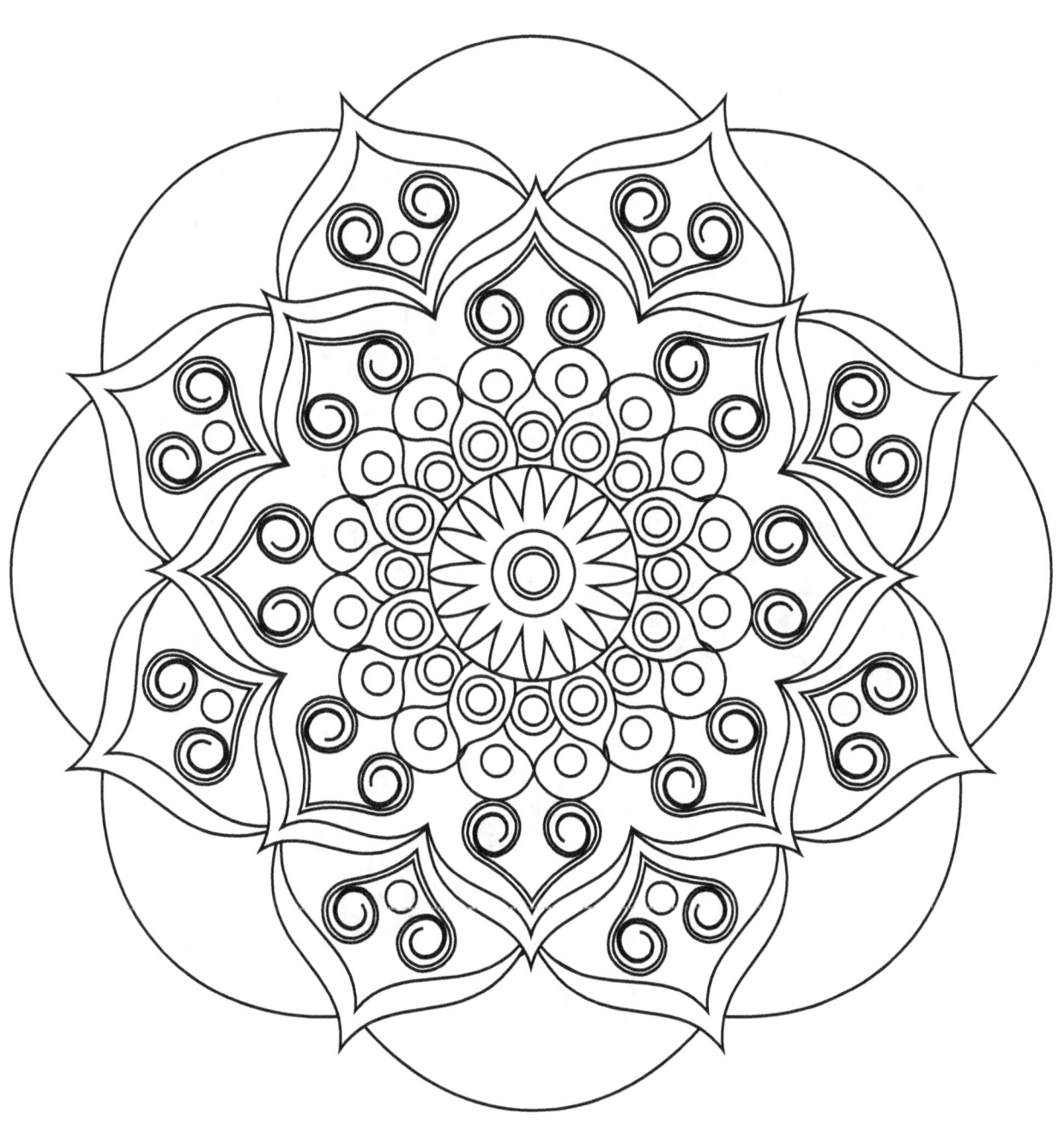

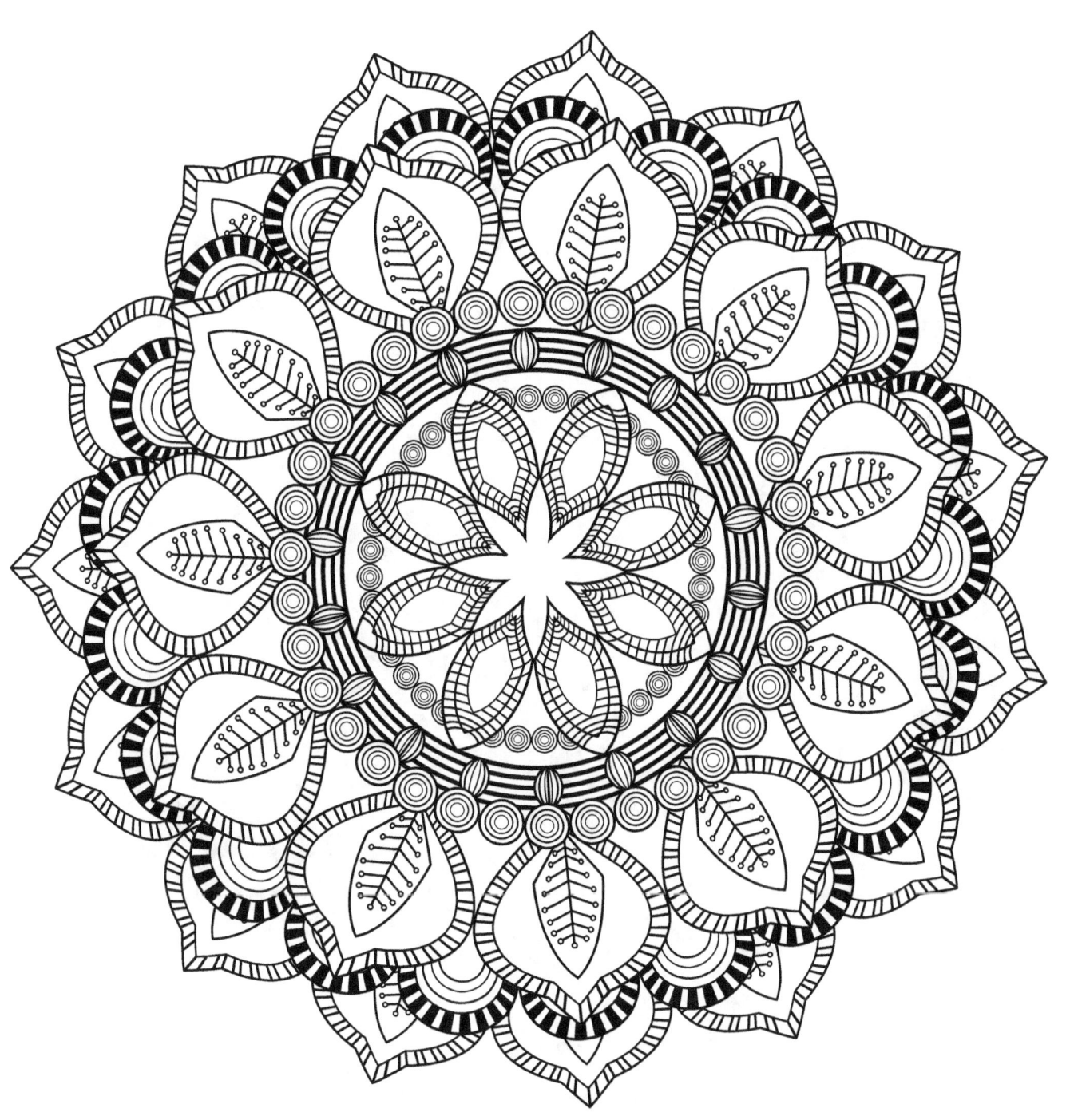

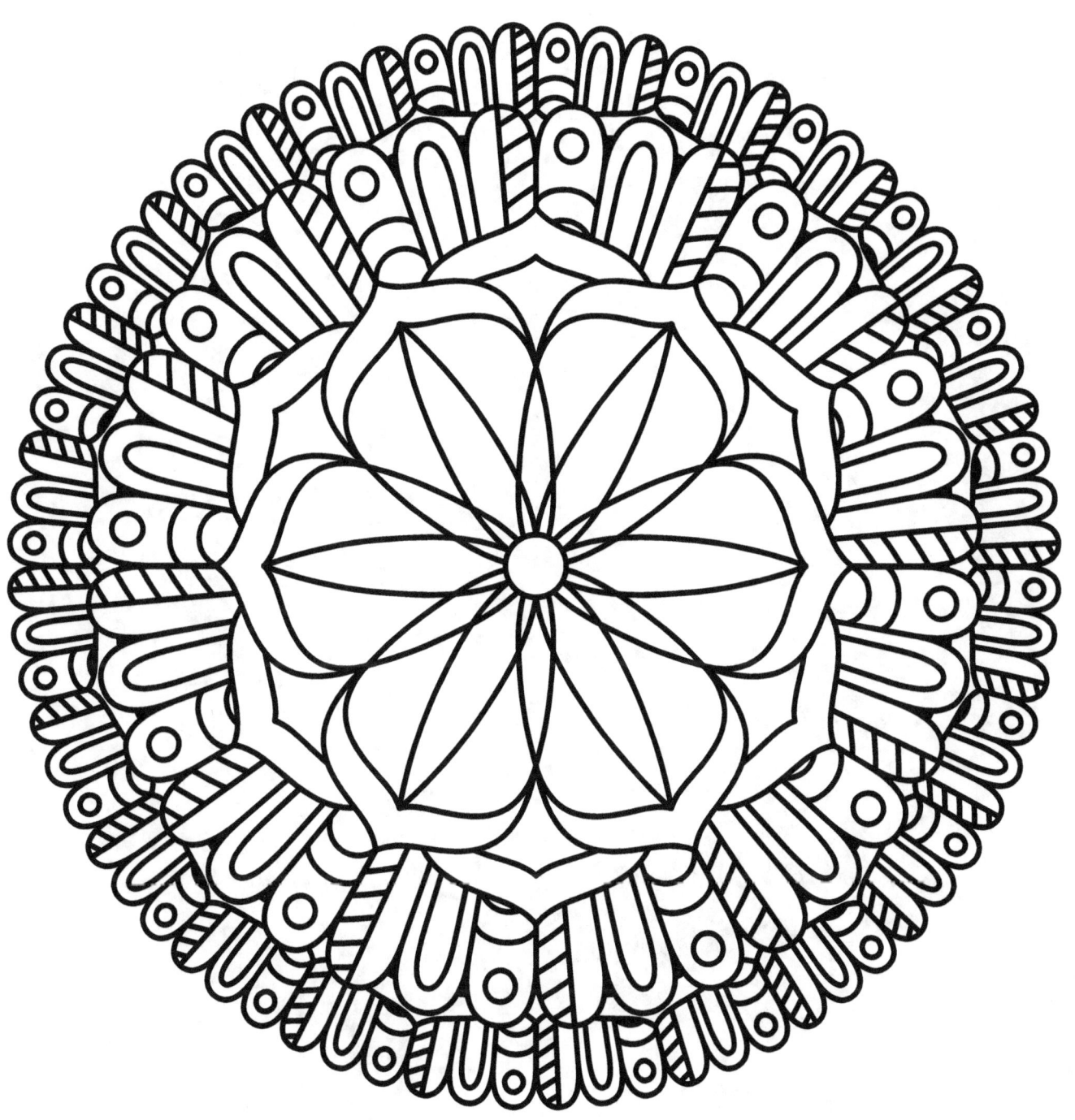

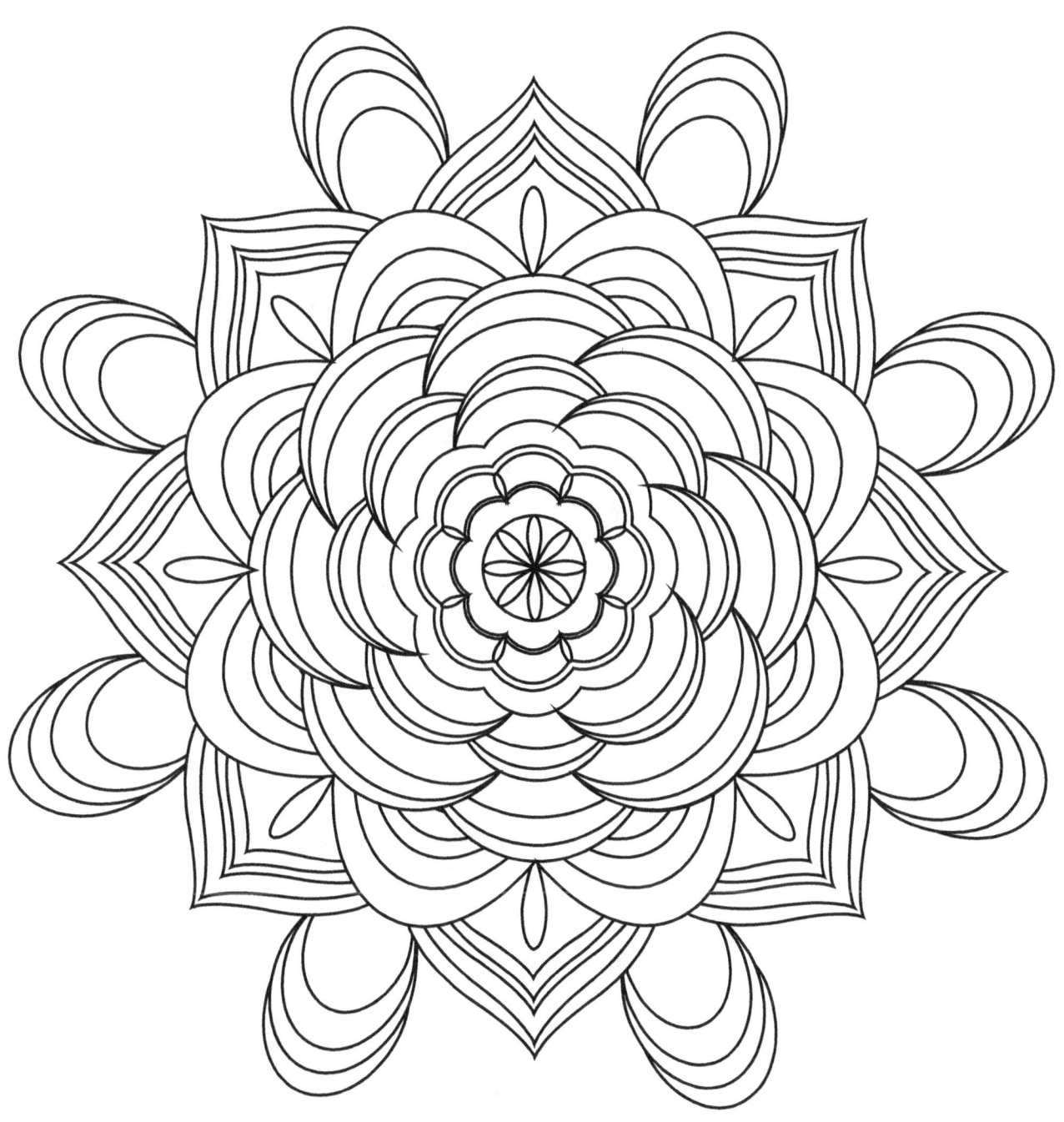

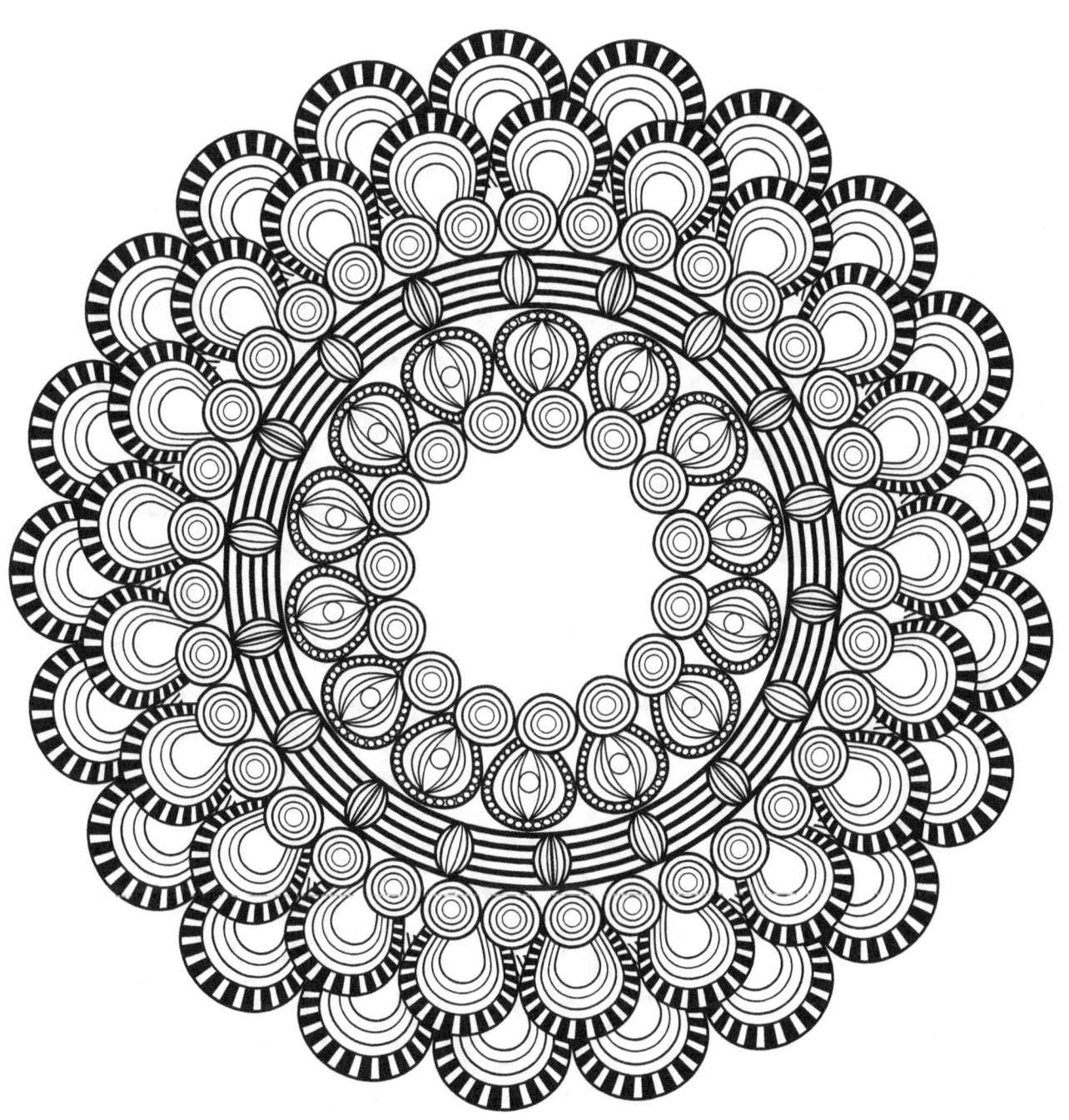

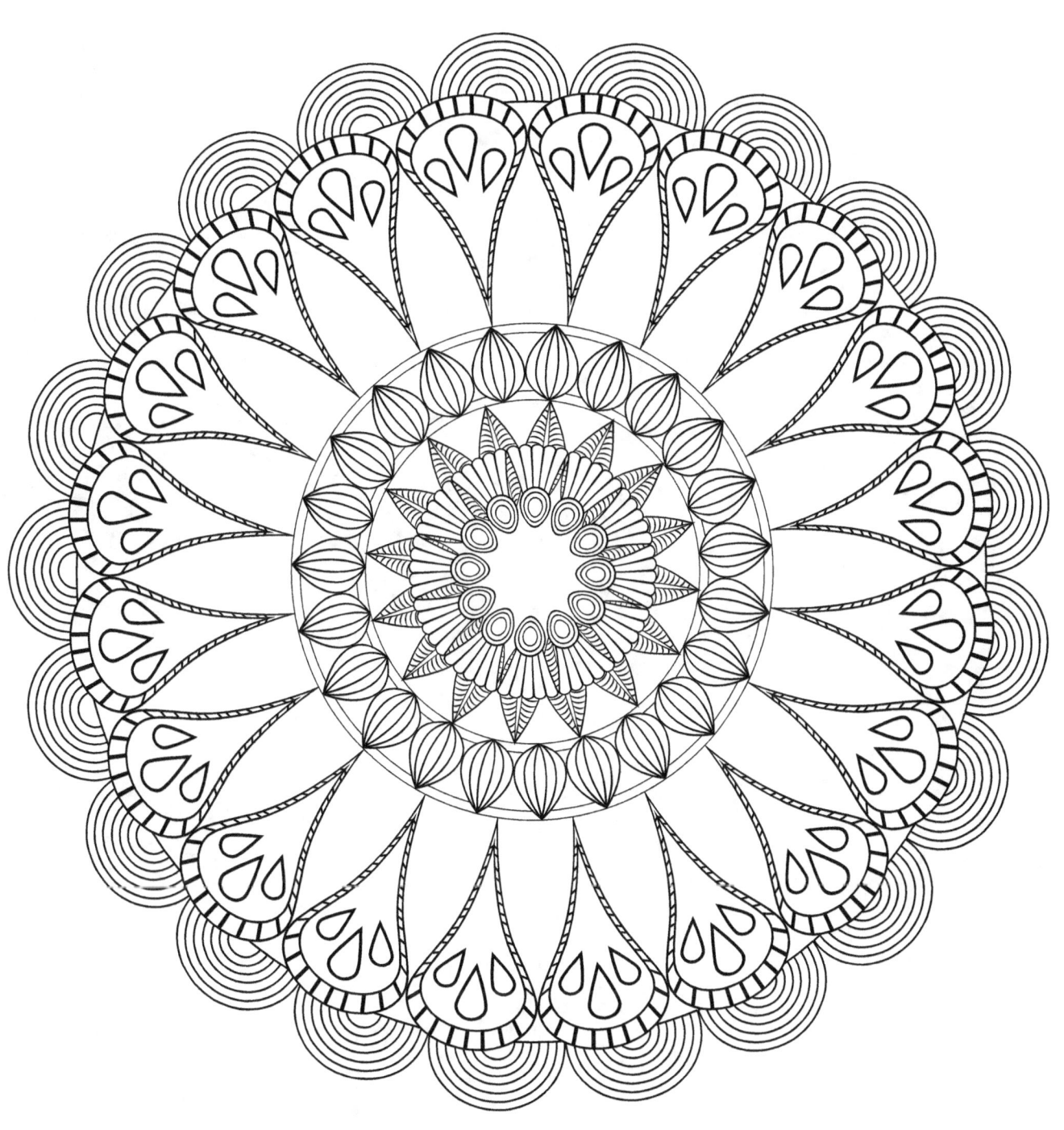

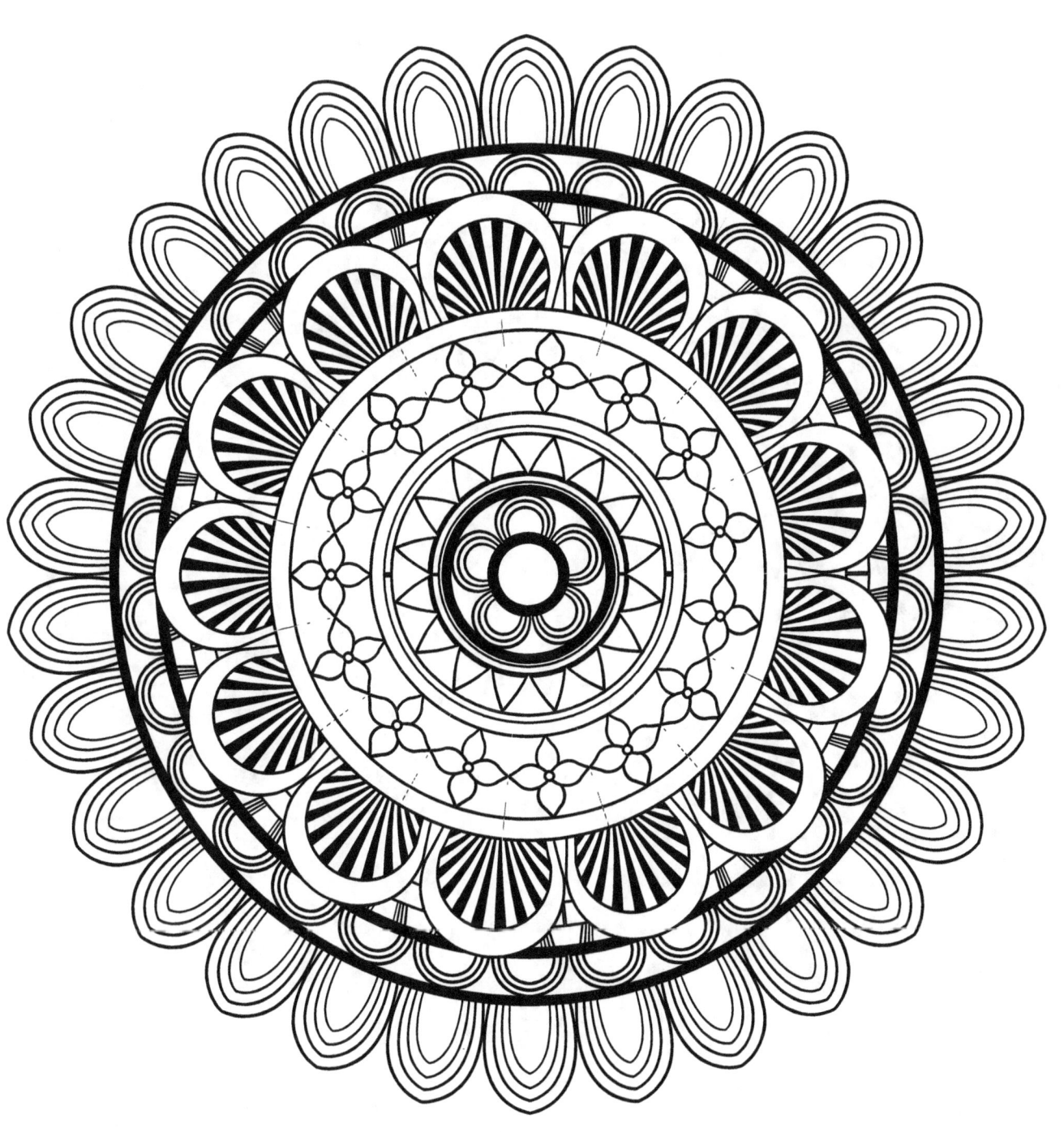

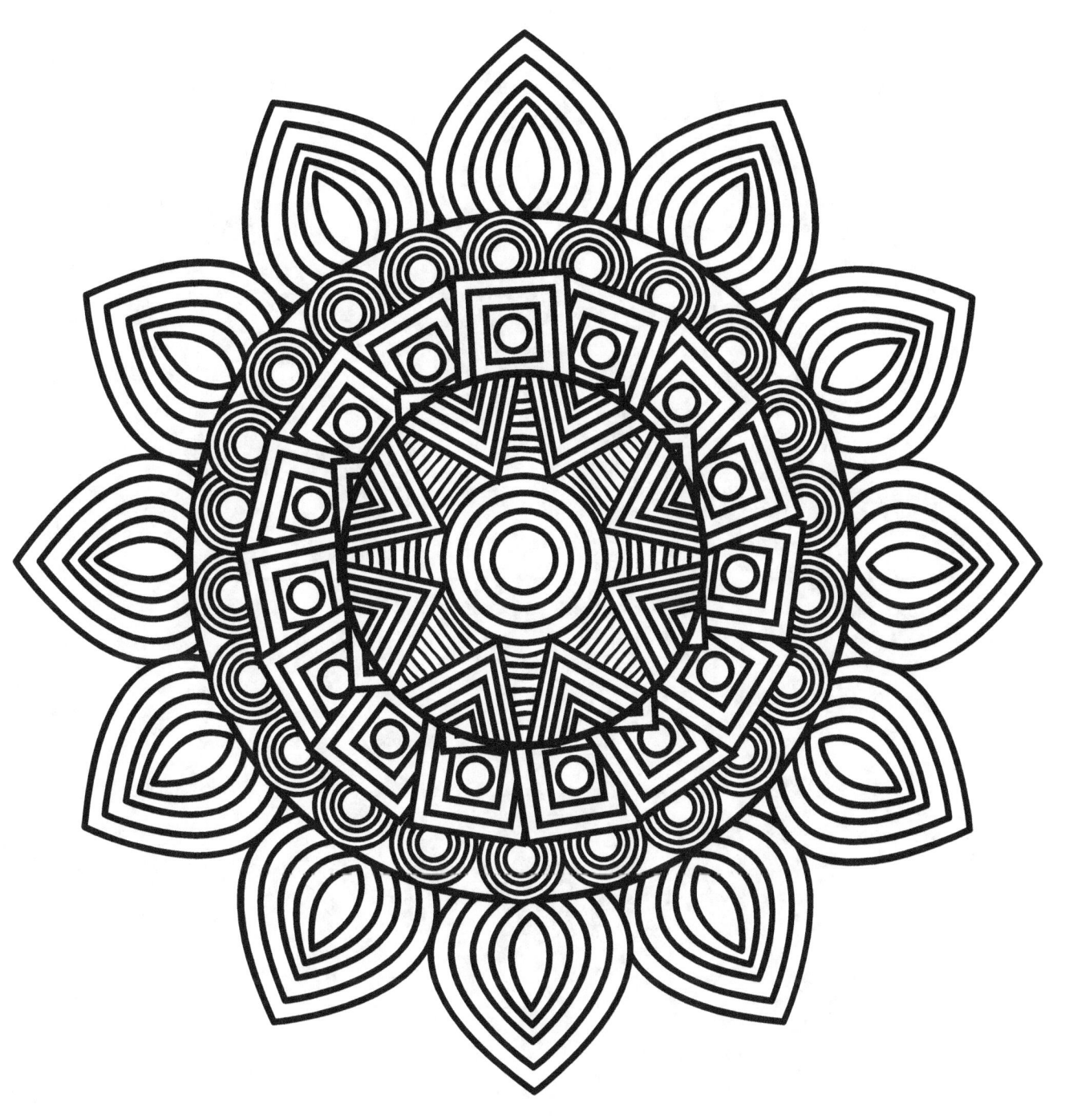

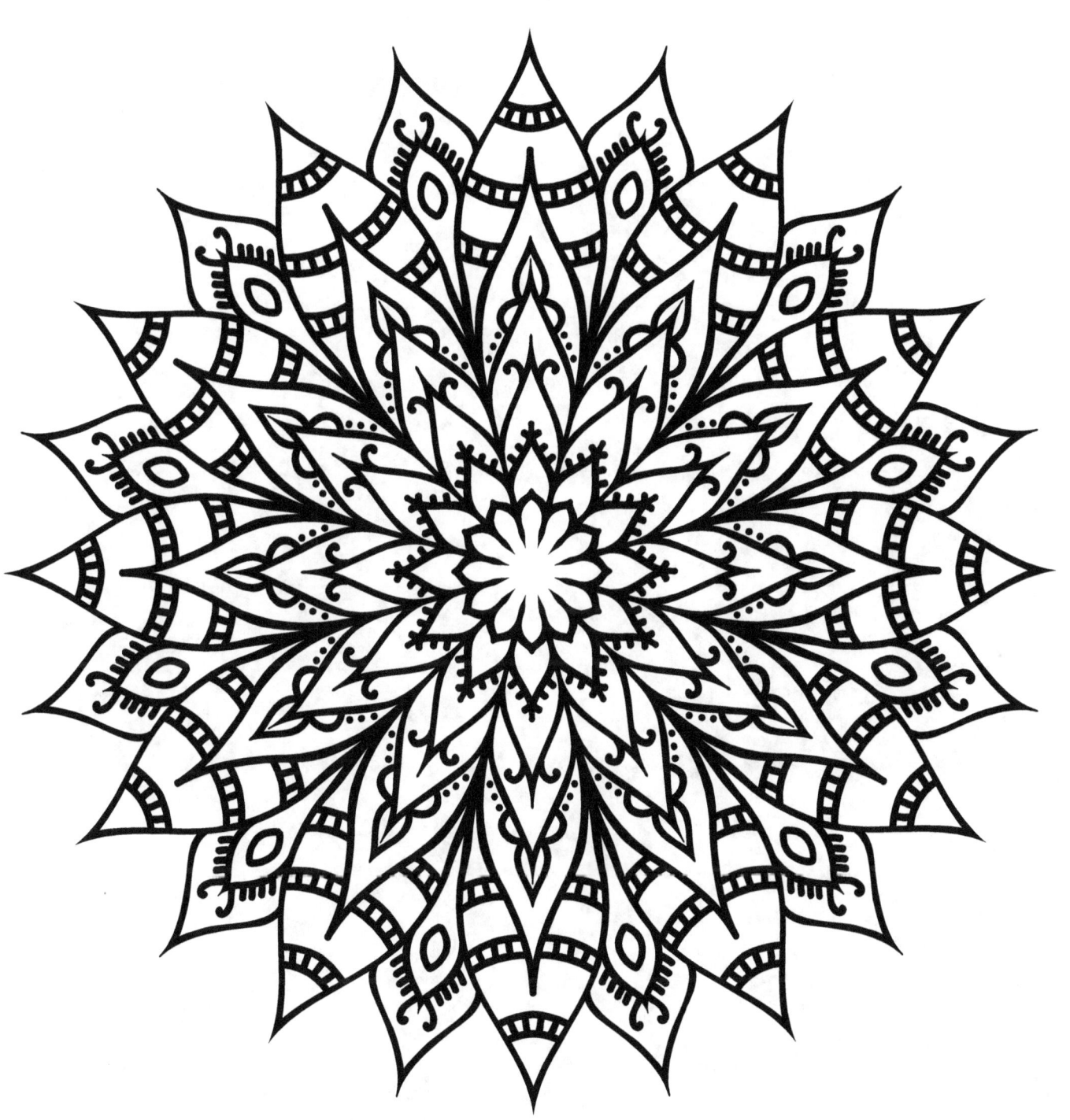

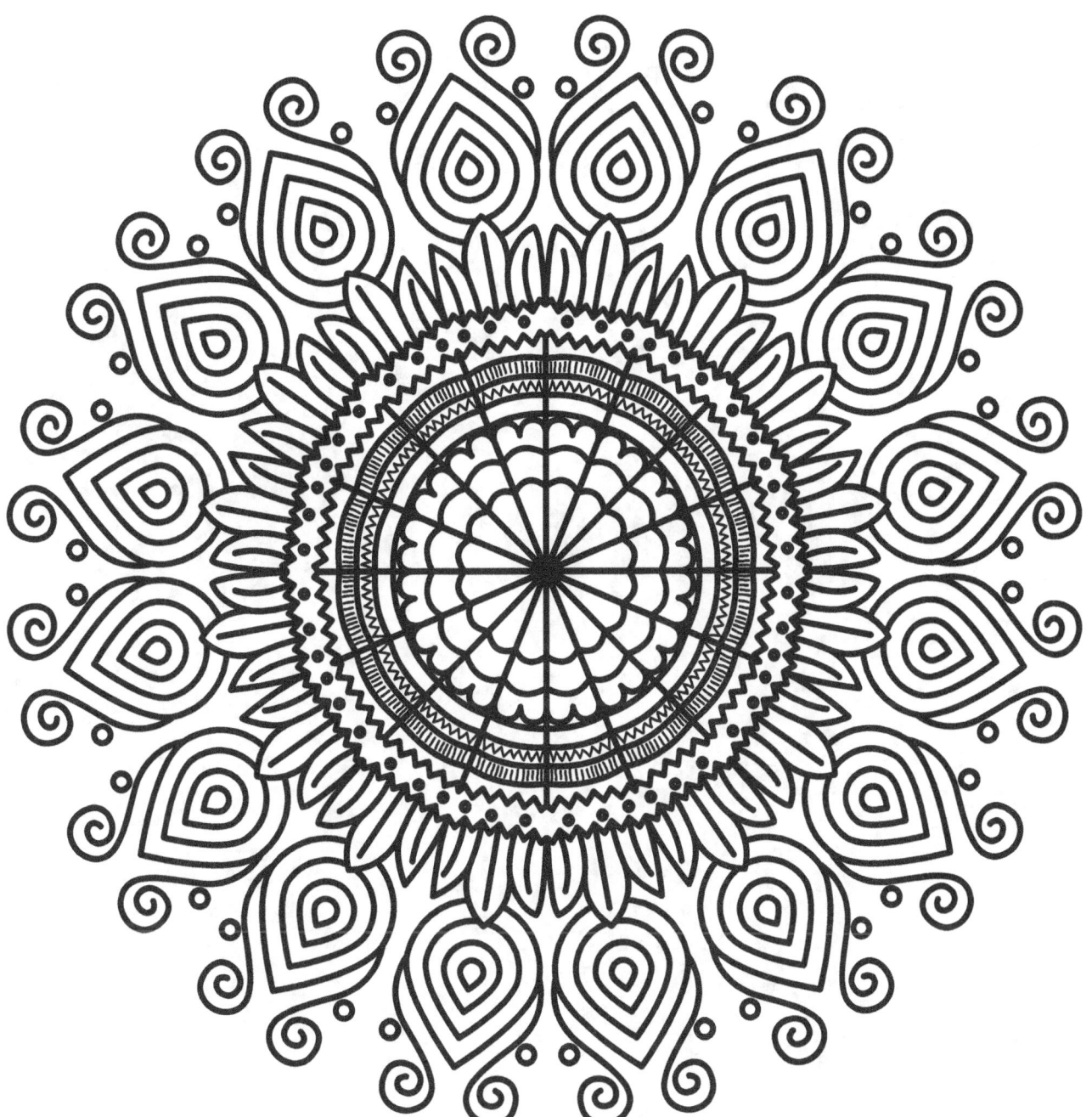

www.ingramcontent.com/pod-product-compliance
Lightning Source LLC
Chambersburg PA
CBHW080504220526
45465CB00006B/2373